Saints Well Seasoned

Saints Well Seasoned

Musings on How Food Nourishes Us:
Body, Heart, and Soul

Edited by
Linda Hoffman Kimball

Deseret Book Company
Salt Lake City, Utah

Cover design by Randall Smith Associates
Cover art, photographic quilt, by Cecily Hunt
Interior illustrations by Linda Hoffman Kimball

Library of Congress Cataloging-in-Publication Data
  Saints well seasoned : musings on how food nourishes us—body, heart, and soul / edited by Linda Hoffman Kimball.
       p.   cm.
    Includes bibliographical references and index.
    ISBN 1-57345-288-2
    1. Christian life—Mormon authors.   2. Food—Religious aspects—Mormon Church.   3. Cookery, American.   I. Kimball, Linda Hoffman.
    BX8656.S25   1998
    248.4'89332—dc21   97-32817
                                                                            CIP

Printed in the United States of America

10   9   8   7   6   5   4   3   2   1   72082

To Christian, Britta, Peter, and Chase, who fill my life with just desserts

CONTENTS

CONTENTS

CONTENTS

CONTENTS

ACKNOWLEDGMENTS

Many thanks to the Deseret Book team and especially to my editor, Emily Watts, who always knew when to tell me to chill and when to turn the heat up. Thanks to my sisters, Holly and Susan, who, although they didn't realize it, were with me every page. Thanks to Diane Brown and Nancy Dredge, who shared their objectivity, professionalism, and good humor. Kudos to my gifted friend Cecily Hunt for the stunning cover art. Thanks to my family, who may wonder, given the theme of this project, why I spent so little time in the kitchen this year. And especially thanks to the willing, good-natured, talented writers who shared their bounty. Bless all the hands that prepared it.

INTRODUCTION

By Linda Hoffman Kimball

This is a book of nourishment. In the following pages you will find an uplifting potluck of essays on one thing we all have in common—food. The writers, all members of The Church of Jesus Christ of Latter-day Saints, share their thoughts on this ordinary (but extraordinary) aspect of life. Through their words we see how food not only feeds the body but enhances community, passes on traditions, puts marrow in the funny bone, and connects us with each other and the Divine.

Mormons are invested in food. Casseroles appear at every birth or passing away. Family recipes tie generations together and make genealogy delicious. Missions challenge many to adapt to new flavors as well as new cultures. Refreshments have drawn flocks in Mormon Country ever since the seagulls found the crickets.

These writers invite you to pull a chair up to the table and join in a reflection and celebration of nourishment, Mormon style.

And Mormon style, you will see, is quite a smorgasbord. This volume presents the talents of a diverse group of men and women. Some are humorists, some fiction writers, some historians, some specialists in English or American literature. Some are poets, journalists, professors, or simply "writers." They come from all over the United States and from Canada. Some are descendants of the pioneers and others are first-generation members of the Church. And, though all are "well seasoned," some have had more years of seasoning than others. Each voice is distinct and adds its own spice to the mix.

One thing these writers share is a gift for words. In these nonfiction pieces they have made common experiences transcendent and extraordinary events accessible to all.

The essays are arranged unlike any other cookbook you will see. There is no "appetizer" category, no "main dish" section. Each piece has its own mood, and reading this book from front to back provides a satisfying blend of tone, texture, and flavor—like a good meal. That's one suggestion. Or you may prefer to leaf through, sampling from here and there. Perfectly acceptable. You may also find yourself returning to favorite portions again and again. That's just fine. It's all you can eat, and no one's checking up on your manners.

However, the nourishment in these pages is not solely literary. Actual recipes are included. Each essay is intentionally limited to "bite-size" length. Following most are related recipes that allow you to share with the authors in a very tangible, even intimate way. In a few cases, the writer's message or style requires that the recipe be incorporated into the body of the text. Please try the recipes that appeal to you, adapt them to your tastes, and share them with your friends. We invite you to participate in this feast.

Saints Well Seasoned may change how you see food. Homemade rolls will become symbols of connection, commitment, and sacrifice. Pork chops will never be the same. Even tuna casserole will take on new dimensions. So dig in, everyone. It's time to eat.

THE SATURDAY
BAKERY

BY DEAN HUGHES

In 1972 my wife, Kathy, and I moved with our two
children to Warrensburg, Missouri. I was fresh out of
grad school and had accepted a teaching job at Central
Missouri State University. As it happened, several other
Mormon professors were hired that same year, and our
families expanded the nucleus of the Saints in the area.
Clearly, it was time to stop renting halls and to build a
church of our own. All we lacked was money.

At that time, local units raised 20 percent of the cost
of a building, which was a huge sum for about forty
families to come up with. We held ward dinners,
brought casseroles, and paid to eat them. We put on
bazaars, made crafts, then bought them. We even held

ward movies and sold ourselves popcorn. One project involved selling fence posts we cut from the limbs of Osage Orange trees. The problem was, we ruined so many chain-saw blades that we were going in the hole.

The task seemed impossible. We could see years ahead of us before construction would start. But one Sunday we held a ward fast and sought guidance in locating a suitable piece of land that we could afford. That week a local physician woke up in the night with the thought that he ought to give us a three-acre parcel of land; he could use the tax deduction.

No one in our ward doubted for a second that a miracle had occurred. Not only did we have our land, but 80 percent of its value was credited to our share of the building costs. We were more than on our way; we could make it now. But it was time for a major push.

What we still needed was to bring in money that wasn't entirely from our own pockets. And that was when Bishop Jim Waite got the idea to open a bakery. He had been a baker in the navy, and a local bakery was sitting idle. He negotiated a deal to use the place on Friday nights and to sell our goods on Saturdays. We called it "The Saturday Bakery." I was a baker, along with Bishop Waite, Jerry Adams, and George Hall. All of us were young, just out of college, and all but George were new to Warrensburg.

Our first night was a near disaster. Either the bishop was a little rusty on his skills or the yeast had lost its kick. The dough sat there and wouldn't "proof." (I learned that word that night.) Time—and some added yeast—finally did get a rise out of the dough, but the sun was up in the morning before we finally took the bread from the ovens. We four bakers stumbled to bed, slept a little, then drove back to find that everything we had baked had sold. And not just to Mormons.

The next week we baked more. In fact, we increased our output every week after that and never completely met the demand. Each Saturday morning—at 3:00 or so—as we bakers finished our work, a clean-up crew would arrive. Before the bakery opened, members of the ward carried in their pies and cakes and cookies and added those to the bread, dinner rolls, and sweet rolls we produced in the bakery. Another crew staffed the store. We weren't getting rich, but it was the best project we had found and virtually everyone was involved.

For many months, the operation continued. We produced hundreds of loaves of bread each week, dozens and dozens of sweet rolls, and our "dead seed rolls." I need to explain these.

One night, when we had been rolling balls of dough for dinner rolls, we were all getting punchy. George, I think it was, was dipping the rolls in sesame seeds when he noticed a little chunk of something black in the bowl. He made the offhand comment, "Hey, there's a dead seed in there." And someone—I promise it wasn't me—said, "These must be dead seed rolls." It was late, and we were all extremely tired. We laughed until we cried, and the name stuck.

We raised money for our church, more by donation than by baking, but the bakery brought in a good deal of money. And I got so I looked forward to those Friday nights. After spending my week with abstractions, I liked producing something by hand—something I could smell and taste, something with heft to it. I also liked the idea that we were producing wholesome food and turning it into a church. But especially, I liked being there with my brothers, laughing and working together.

We built our church. And finally the day came to move in. That same week, George Hall's six-year-old daughter, Stephanie, was hit by a pickup truck and killed. Before we had a chance to hold a ward dinner to celebrate our achievement, we held a funeral in our beloved new building.

In our small ward little Stephie had seemed a daughter to all of us, so everyone felt the grief. We gathered around George and Ginny and tried to share their burden. I'll always remember a day, a month or two after the funeral, when George, quietly and stoically, told me what he was feeling. Men don't talk as openly as we should, and we aren't very good at expressing our love, but I felt our bond that day. After, when we needed to laugh, we reminisced about the bakery, and we joked about the dead seed rolls.

Every now and then I walk into a bakery and smell the baking bread—and it all comes back to me: The Saturday Bakery, the church we built, little Stephie. I think of my brother bakers, the exhaustion, and the devotion we had to our cause. I find myself longing for that kind of challenge again, just so I can feel that close to a group of people one more time. I know that I—along with everyone who shared those challenges—am better for the experience. Our love "proofed" the wholesome ingredients, and we made something fine out of the pain we all shared.

I'm also glad I've been a baker. I feel I learned the value, the goodness, even the meaning of bread. I love ideas, and I love bread, but in that bakery we put the two together, and it was the best food I ever tasted.

Dolly's Rolls

These are not the rolls we made in the bakery, but a great, simple recipe my wife's mother passed along to all of us in the family.

1 package active dry yeast
1¼ cups warm water
1¼ cups evaporated milk
⅓ cup sugar
2 eggs, beaten
1 teaspoon salt
6 tablespoons vegetable oil
6 cups flour

In a large bowl, dissolve yeast in water; add evaporated milk, sugar, and beaten eggs. Mix well. Add salt, oil, and enough of the flour to make a soft dough. (Dolly believed it was better to use slightly less than the 6 cups.) Cover bowl and let dough rise until doubled in bulk. Roll dough out on a lightly floured board. Shape into rolls as desired; let rise again. Bake at 350 degrees F. for about 20 minutes or until golden brown. Makes approximately 2½ dozen.

Add sesame seeds if desired—but watch out for dead seeds!

IN CAMILLA'S KITCHEN

BY EDWARD L. KIMBALL

When my mother, Camilla, died, we divided up her belongings. Among the things I chose for myself was her file box of three-by-five-inch recipe cards. Thumbing through them takes me back to mother-as-cook.

Born in 1894, she was by training and choice a homemaker. As a young woman she taught home economics at the LDS Church academies in Hinckley, Utah, and Thatcher, Arizona, and even had a plan to study dietetics at Johns Hopkins University, until marriage intervened and made her own kitchen the focus of her skills. A great cook, she offered nothing fancy in her meals, but they satisfied. Her father said her cooking was "salubrious!" and, since her mother's cooking was notably not, he liked to eat at Camilla's. He said, "Nothing Camilla cooks ever bothers my stomach."

Leftovers posed no problem. The remainders of Sunday's roast or other dish appeared on successive days in a variety of forms, all tasty. By about Thursday, any remnant was likely to appear as an ingredient in corn fritters. The road ended there.

Mother's ideas about child rearing reflected the notions of the day. She had read that refined sugar would ferment in the stomach, and so the children were not allowed to have sugar on their morning cracked-wheat cereal. But my father had sugar on his.

Though Dad worked at a white-collar job in our small town, we had some livestock at home—always a cow or two, sometimes chickens, pigs, a sheep—and a garden. Mother set milk from the cows out in pans for the cream to rise. She then kept it in a small crock in the refrigerator until she was ready to make butter. Sometimes she would take a crust of bread and scoop up some of the clotted cream as a treat—for her, not for the children, although she was not always looking. Eventually we bought a separator and spun out the cream and sold it to the local creamery for welcome cash. We ate creamed vegetables, but drank a lot of blue milk.

The kitchen table served as the center of the home. There we studied our lessons, played games, ate meals. We settled the frequent arguments about words by recourse to the dictionary that was always within arm's reach of the table.

Until the last few of her ninety-two years, Camilla did her own cooking and cleaning, with occasional help from her only daughter. When any of her three sons came to visit, they were sure to look soon in the refrigerator and find something good—hunger had little to do with the search. She loved to work in her yard, tending flowers and her vegetable garden, fruit trees and bushes. She canned as a normal activity even after the effort could not be justified in monetary terms.

Camilla discarded nothing that could be repaired for use again in its own or some other form. She came by her sense of thrift honestly. Her own mother's experience had included times of real hunger, so she grew up with the tradition "waste not, want not." Camilla shopped the sales and went from store to store buying loss leaders. She instilled thrift in her children to a large degree, with much passing on to the grandchildren—at least to some of the grandchildren.

She brought home food she had not eaten on airplane flights or at banquets she attended. A memorable moment in frugality occurred the day Mother gave a wedding shower for one of her granddaughters and found, left over from preparation of the fruit salad she had served, watermelon rinds. She decided then that the rinds need not be thrown away; they could be pickled. And pickle them she did.

But watermelon pickles were just one sort. No festive dinner was complete without an array—sweet and dill cucumber pickles, relish, watermelon pickles, pick-led beets. I love the dark red crunch of pickled beets. Today when I go to a salad bar I always try the beets even though I know that usually they're not pickled, they're just . . . beets. And if they are pickled, the taste is bland. What I need are beets with a little bite. When I do find them, they bring back sharp memories of childhood Thanksgiving and Christmas.

We looked forward eagerly to baking days, when we could come home from school to the tempting aroma of fresh bread and cinnamon rolls, dough spread thin, filled generously with raisins, cinnamon, and brown sugar. No one has ever made them better than my mother. I hear such pastries called "sticky buns," but in my lexicon that would demean them. They're properly "cinnamon rolls."

Grandfather was right; those who sat at my mother's table enjoyed truly salubrious eating.

WATERMELON PICKLES

1 large, firm watermelon
Sugar
Salt (noniodized)
Alum
Vinegar
2 teaspoons whole cloves
2 cinnamon sticks (whole)
1 teaspoon ground mace
1 small orange, thinly sliced
1 small lemon, thinly sliced
Additional whole cloves
12 to 15 pint jars

Wash watermelon and peel with carrot peeler. Cut melon into 1½-inch slices; then cut each slice in half. Scoop out fruit for other use, leaving some pink on the rind. Cut rind with grooved cutter to make large, diamond-shaped pieces.

Weigh rind and set aside an equal weight of sugar. Place rind in a large kettle and add water to cover, measuring how much water you use. Add 1 tablespoon noniodized salt for each quart water used. Let stand overnight.

Bring to a boil. Boil gently 45 minutes and drain.

Cover rind with cold water again, adding 2 tablespoons alum per quart of water.

Boil 45 minutes, drain, and rinse well.

Cover with same amount of cold water as previously used.

Boil 45 minutes.

Add sugar and boil 45 minutes.

Add ⅓ cup vinegar for each cup water used. Tie cloves, cinnamon, and mace in a cheesecloth bag and add to kettle.

Boil 45 minutes and then discard spices.

As soon as pickles finish cooking, put thin slice of orange on bottom of each clean, hot jar. Pack hot pickles into jar, put lemon slice and two whole cloves on top, fill with hot syrup, and process to seal.

Makes 12 to 15 pints.

CAMILLA'S CINNAMON ROLLS

1 tablespoon butter or other fat

1 tablespoon salt

¾ cup dry milk

½ cup honey

½ cup sugar (optional, for a sweeter dough)

1 tablespoon molasses

6 cups water

6 cups flour (half whole wheat, if desired)

1 package active dry yeast

¼ cup warm water

Butter

Brown sugar

Cinnamon

Raisins

Chopped pecans

Mix together butter or other fat, salt, dry milk, honey, sugar (if desired), molasses, 6 cups water, and 2 cups of the flour. Soften yeast in ¼ cup warm water; add to batter and allow to rest a few minutes.

Add remaining 4 cups flour and mix, adding more flour if needed to make a moderately stiff dough that does not stick to the sides of the mixing bowl. More flour is needed in humid climate.

Put dough in buttered mixing bowl, cover with slightly damp cloth, and place in warm spot to rise. When dough is doubled in size, punch it down, knead it lightly in bowl, and let rise again. Turn dough onto floured surface, knead thoroughly, and roll out into thin rectangle.

Spread generously with butter, brown sugar, cinnamon, raisins, and chopped pecans. Repeat; the first time was not enough. Roll up from long end and pinch dough to seal. Cut into one-inch segments.

Butter two 13 x 9-inch pans generously and spread with brown sugar. Arrange rolls in pans. Bake at 350 degrees F. for 25 to 30 minutes or until golden. Turn over onto cookie sheet, exposing caramelized sugar. Makes approximately 5 dozen rolls.

FROM BAYOU TO
BEEHIVE:
A GASTRONOMIC
GENEALOGY

BY KATHRYN H. KIDD

I don't remember my childhood. I once watched a
two-hour videotape of home movies without recognizing it was filmed in the home where I had lived until I
was eleven. Nobody has to prod me about my culinary
heritage, however. I have Technicolor memories of the
food I ingested as a child. Not all of it was pleasant, but
no autobiography is without its share of tragedies.

My maternal grandmother died young, leaving my
mother to grow up with a housekeeper whose cooking

skills were widely renowned. Botchie produced comfort food, and her talent was so extraordinary that there are family recipes I refuse to give out because I haven't given up the idea of mass-producing them and selling them. I'm never going to get rich as a novelist, but Botchie's baked beans could make my fortune. If only I weren't too lazy to market them.

Mother's comfort-food stage lasted until she was orphaned at the age of twelve. She was taken in by an uncle and aunt who had grown up in Southern Louisiana—Cajun country. Aunt Mayme was a Cajun cook, when she cooked at all. Her stuffed cabbage was a work of art. But usually the cooks did the work. That's "cooks," plural. A big head cook got the credit, but a bunch of little auxiliary cooks yapped at the head cook's heels. This team of chefs was responsible for preparing food for the four people who lived in my uncle's household. The head cook was dearer to me than most of my blood relatives. When my sister called a few years back, sobbing because Eddie was dead, the depth of her grief told me it was Eddie the cook who had died, rather than Ed our father or even Eddie, my sister's own husband.

Although they lived in Mississippi, Eddie and her assistant cooks prepared traditional French cuisine. Mother reveled in the food, but she did not feel the need to learn any lessons from the resident chefs. When she married and moved to New Orleans, she had no clue how to cook. She covered this deficiency by drowning everything she cooked in stewed tomatoes and oregano. Back then, oregano wasn't as refined as it is now. Today *oregano* means leaves; in the 1950s, there were more twigs than leaves in a bottle of oregano. I grew up hating the idea of having to dig sticks out of everything that was put on my plate and eat around the tomato goop besides. To this day, my sisters and I detest Italian food in any form.

My father's idea of cooking was foreign to that of my mother. He had grown up in a poor family on the Texas-Mexico border, and anything he prepared had its own flavor. He had a way with turnip greens, and it was his influence that inspired me to add jalapeños to tuna fish and scrambled eggs. Most of the food that came from his side of the family was remarkable only for its badness, though. When I commented on dishes my paternal grandmother cooked, I first had to surreptitiously find out what I was eating. My sister once remarked on the "interesting peanut butter pie," only to be told in frosty tones that she was consuming butterscotch.

One of the breakfast mainstays of my childhood must have come from my father. It was called "stirred-up," and it consisted of huge globs of real butter, peanut butter, and maple syrup stirred together on a plate with a knife. Etiquette demanded that stirred-up be eaten with a knife unless the one who was doing the eating preferred to sop it up with slice after slice of white bread. Stirred-up was the first thing I learned how to "cook" and is probably the reason that since I have reached adulthood, I have refused to eat peanuts in any form. (Readers who want to simulate the taste of stirred-up can do so by consuming the orange part of a Butterfingers candy bar, without the chocolate. Now imagine eating two cups of that for breakfast.)

Growing up in New Orleans added its own flavor to my culinary ancestry. I was weaned on soft-shell crabs and raw oysters, kumquats and mirlitons, anchovies and étouffée. I miss crawfish with a longing that most people feel after the death of a beloved pet. I order muffaletta sandwiches whenever I see them on a menu, but they're never authentic, and I'm always disappointed.

The cuisines of my heritage make me Comfort-Cajun-French-Oregano-Texican-New Orleanian, in more or less equal parts. To say that I suffered culinary culture shock when I adopted Mormonism is an understatement. But I've never done things halfway, so I learned to eat like a Mormon—with all the baggage that entails. There's Ward Dinner Cooking, where women prepare things their families would never eat at home. There's Food Storage Cooking, with recipes that incorporate the weevily delights and bottled surprises that are sitting in the corner of the family basement. Then there's the apex of Mormon cooking—the art practiced by those celestial beings who are nearing translation: Bread Making. (Pause for a moment of reverent contemplation.)

I've been through all the stages. I was a starving student at BYU, joining the hordes of young people who ate bleu cheese dressing with their fingertips to stave off hunger pangs at lunch. There were so many of us that the compassionate soul who managed the Cougareat started charging for salad dressing. After that there was nothing to do but to make tomato soup out of catsup or to fast. I preferred fasting.

After our marriage, Clark and I became Word of Wisdom fanatics. We ground whole wheat flour for a year, until we realized that Clark's system just couldn't tolerate it. We were vegetarians for about a month. We didn't eat white sugar for a long time, and I was so diligent about our conversion that I threw away all my cherished recipes. (I'd kill to get those recipes back!) We made our own mayonnaise until we got tired of finding spatula bits in our sandwiches. Needless to say, we've done the bread bit. We still eat very few processed foods.

When we lived in Utah, Clark and I were the home-canning king and queen of North America. We bottled everything from sliced mushrooms to jalapeño baked beans. Once we won second prize in a canning contest at the Utah State Fair for creating a recipe of bottled fruit bread. First prize was fifty dollars. Second prize was one dollar. We never cashed our check.

Winning that red ribbon whetted my appetite for culinary competition. I began entering our ward's annual cake-baking contest. Usually I won. The last time I entered, I later learned that when I was announced as the winner, one of the other women said, "I'm not going to clap for her. She *always* wins. She only uses the finest of ingredients." When I wrote my first novel, *Paradise Vue,* I added a chapter about a ward dinner just so I could put that story in the text.

Ironically, cake baking has never been one of my strengths. I only prevailed against the competition because my cakes were different from everyone else's. I didn't use mixes or shortening or margarine. I didn't frost my cakes with Cool Whip or put them in dripper pans to maximize the number of servings that one cake could yield. I didn't produce *Utah* cakes, and the judges rewarded me for my conspicuous departure from local tradition.

Just as I can't produce Utah cakes, I can't replicate the cooking of any of the Mormons around me. I may be able to *eat* like them, but I've never learned to cook like them. I have a confession to make: I can't get Jello to harden, I can't stomach iceberg lettuce, and I'm not quite sure what casseroles involve. My food is usually the first to go at a ward dinner, not because I'm a *good* cook, but because I'm a *different* one.

Spiritually, I'm a Mormon in every cell of my body. Culinarily, however, I'm forever exiled to the fringes of my adopted religion. My spirit is willing to join the faithful at the center of culinary American Mormonism, but my taste buds are invariably weak.

SUSIE'S BARBECUED SHRIMP

1½ cups butter (not margarine!)
1 tablespoon lemon juice
35-60 drops Tabasco sauce
2 teaspoons salt
1 teaspoon pepper
¼ teaspoon oregano leaves
1 bay leaf, crushed
1 bunch garlic (a whole, huge head of it, coarsely
    chopped)
3 pounds headless shrimp
4 ears of corn
4 baguettes (long, thin loaves of French bread)

In a saucepan, combine butter, lemon juice, Tabasco sauce, salt, pepper, oregano, bay leaf, and chopped garlic; heat until butter melts. Pour over shrimp in a large casserole dish. Add corn. Place in refrigerator and marinate overnight. Cook, uncovered, at 350 degrees F. for twenty minutes or so, stirring often. Serve with bread to dip in the butter. Serves 4.

THREE-MINUTE COBBLER

½ cup butter (not margarine!)
¾ cup milk
¼ teaspoon salt
2 teaspoons baking powder
1 cup sugar
1 cup flour
Fruit for filling

Melt butter over low heat in an 8-inch square casserole dish. Stir in remaining ingredients. The mixture will be lumpy. Don't sweat it. Then pour in—DO NOT STIR!—1 medium can fruit for pies or canned pie filling, or bottled, drained fruit, or sliced, fresh fruit, or sweetened, frozen fruit. Bake at 350 degrees F. for about 50 minutes, or until the cobbler is puffy and brown on top. Serve hot or cold, with or without whipped cream or ice cream. Serves 4.

How to Kill
a Turkey

By Berniece Rabe

My husband's mother died shortly before we were married, so I wanted to make sure he had his family's traditional Thanksgiving Feast. We had so little money, I felt it my job to shop wisely and stretch those pennies my husband earned at his factory job. When I saw an ad in the paper for turkey, 27 cents a pound, live weight, I yelled, "Fantastic! I'll get the turkey cheap." So what if I had to buy it live. At least we'd know it was fresh. I had killed chickens on the farm in Missouri when I was growing up. I had even scalded, plucked, and dressed them. This would be no problem.

The man on the turkey farm was a bit aghast when

I said, "Would you put the turkey in the back of the car on the floor, please?"

He didn't tell me that his customers did pay live weight, but that *he* usually killed the turkey and dressed it. He just shrugged at my peculiarity (my Missouri farm accent was still pretty thick back then), tied the feet of the big bird, and put it in the car.

To the loud music of gobbling, I drove home.

My husband had just been dropped off from work. He rushed to open my car door. Then he backed away, shocked.

"We saved a lot of money," I said. That eased him somewhat. I stood back and admired how he was able to lift that big fellow out of the car and tie it to a tree.

Because we were recent converts, the only Latter-day Saints in our town, we would do right by the missionaries this holiday. We invited them over. Come Thanksgiving Day, the elders arrived very early. I was so glad, for my husband had to rush back to his work that morning because of some emergency, and I needed that turkey killed.

"It's too big for me to wring its neck," I explained. "But I already have a five-gallon drum of water ready to scald it and loosen its feathers so I can pluck it."

The elders seemed shocked. But they'd been counseled to work with the culture of the people they taught, and one bravely began to discuss how the job could be accomplished.

"I'm not about to chop its head off," declared the other loudly.

The gobbles grew louder too.

The first elder, who was rather small framed, said, "Sister Rabe, do you have a straight-edge razor?"

"No," I answered a bit indignantly. "My father used those old-fashioned razors, but my husband sure doesn't."

"Well, just bring me whatever razor your husband uses," he said to me. He explained to his protesting companion, "I may not be able to chop its head off, but at least I can cut the jugular."

I raced inside the house and was out in a flash handing this cooperative elder a tiny Schick Injector razor blade. Again, he stood in shock. But he was determined to meet the challenges of his mission, so he dashed toward that angry bird.

He didn't even come close before the wing-stretched bird made him retreat. Again he tried. And again. Who knows how it would have ended if my twenty-three-year-old husband hadn't returned from the factory just then and showed those nineteen-year-old missionaries what to do.

Later I learned that my husband was plenty scared too, but at the time he just sounded very in-charge as he ordered the two missionaries around. He told them to help him catch the bird, tie its feet, and hold its wings. Then he got an ax and a piece of firewood. Whack! Whack! Whack! Quite pale and with a great look of relief, he handed me the bird to scald.

Sometimes I think he still wonders just who he married.

Well, at the time, he was married to a tender, loving, and compassionate nineteen-year-old who had gotten his mother's recipe for German stuffing to put inside that big bird. I'd like to say it was a wonderful Thanksgiving dinner we had that day, and I could say that—had not one protesting elder kept verbalizing all during the dinner how we would have to face that scrappy bird at the judgment bar and apologize for taking its life. However, we have had many great Thanksgivings since.

I found it so much simpler when I could go to the supermarket and find on sale a nice clean bird all ready to be stuffed, one I'd never had any confrontation with, one I was not even sure had ever gobbled or had a great wing and tail span with feathers so beautiful they'd be saved to make my future children a great tribal headdress. Still, I can't forget our first Thanksgiving, for it was the first time I ever made German dressing.

German Dressing

Turkey neck and giblets
1 loaf of stale stuffing bread, torn into small pieces
6 tart apples, coarsely chopped
1 cup raisins or chopped prunes
½ teaspoon cinnamon
¼ teaspoon anise
1 teaspoon salt
2 tablespoons sugar

    Place turkey neck and giblets in 4-quart pan. Cover with water and cook until tender. Mix remaining ingredients in large bowl. Remove meat from the neck and chop the giblets. Add them and the broth to the bread mixture. Then stuff the bird and bake until tender and golden.

Invite the missionaries. They may be surprised but not shocked. The aroma will win them instantly.

RICE CHRISTIANS

BY MARY ELLEN EDMUNDS

I want to be known as a Rice Christian. It is a phrase I heard a lot during my years working in Southeast Asia, though it was never said in a positive way. It was used to describe someone who joined a particular religious group hoping for rice or other material handouts. It was as if the person had no strong connection to Jesus Christ, and any "conversion" was a matter of the stomach, not the heart. But did we miss something when we used that term? Was there something deeply symbolic in the need for rice? Have I ever been that hungry, that desperate, that I could understand such a thing?

Growing up, I always liked rice in almost any form, but we didn't eat it very often. Mostly it was something we had instead of potatoes from time to time, or part of what we got when we ordered Chinese food. We sometimes had rice pudding, and there were occasions where I saw someone throw rice at a newly married couple.

In 1962 I had my first encounter with rice as the focal point of every meal. In Asia, rice was much more than a side dish or a substitute for anything else, and I don't remember ever seeing it thrown at anyone for any reason. Everything else in the meal supplemented or complemented the fluffy white heaps of *bigas* or *nasi* or whatever it might be called in different places. It was the center of subsistence, and for some families it seemed to be the "glue of the day."

Rice in Asia isn't a *package,* it is a *process.* It is the Law of the Harvest up close and personal. Even those who bought it in the market from huge baskets (priced according to how many rocks and other impurities were left for personal removal at home) knew the process very well.

I have watched people standing in water planting the rice seedlings. I've seen the extraordinary network of waterways on the sides of hills in Taiwan, the Philippines, Indonesia, and other places, with the beautiful distinct green indicating that the tiny plants are beginning to grow in their water beds. I remember watching a man in Hong Kong carefully watering his rice paddies with two watering cans balanced on the ends of a bamboo pole across his shoulders. I've observed the beautiful green fields turn to the ripened color of mature rice.

I've had a chance to watch the harvesting process,

again done by hand. And I've seen all the stacks of rice for sale in the open marketplace. I remember feeling like a little child as I waited for the "Puffed Rice Man" to come in Taiwan. We would take our little bag of rice out to him, and he'd heat it up and shoot it out of a very simple, old-fashioned cannon.

One experience that helped me understand the value of rice—of even one grain of rice—happened in a refugee camp in Thailand. During a visit to a home, I was enjoying watching some children play in the small area in front of the shelter. One of them accidentally knocked a bag of rice over, and some of the rice spilled. I watched the family pick up every grain of rice and put it back in the bag—and I thought of how many grains of rice I've wasted.

In Indonesia I learned of the consecration of members of the local branch to which I belonged in Central Java. The Relief Society president, Ibu Subowo, had invited each member to save in a plastic bag one spoonful of uncooked rice before beginning to prepare food in the morning. Relief Society was held on Saturdays then, and each sister would bring her small bag of rice, her holy contribution to someone in need. I wonder what the equivalent would be for me if I were to try to make such a donation.

Saints of various religions shared rice with me many times. They gave their rice as an offering of love and friendship, connection and esteem, from their hearts to mine. Sometimes we ate with chopsticks and sometimes with fingers. It's not as easy to eat rice with a fork or even a spoon. These people shared generously and tenderly from their often meager stores. I was aware of one family who skipped several meals in order to share some rice with us. I'm sure this happened on other occasions but was kept a secret.

In their sharing of this most basic of gifts, this rice, I was nourished spiritually and physically. I have memories connected with the fluffy white stuff—sometimes with rocks and other additions—that cannot be erased from my heart. For the most part, those memories are connected to unselfish brothers and sisters with kind, brown faces and dark, gentle eyes—my fellow Rice Christians.

Nasi Goreng (Indonesian Fried Rice)

2 medium onions, chopped
3 tablespoons olive oil
4 cups cooked rice (leftovers are fine)
1 cup chopped cooked ham
2 teaspoons curry powder
¼ teaspoon ground coriander
¼ teaspoon ground cumin
¼ teaspoon salt
1 can (5 ounces) tiny shrimp, drained
2 tablespoons snipped fresh parsley

In a large frying pan or wok, stir onions in oil over medium heat until tender. Add rice, ham, and spices. Cook and stir until rice is golden brown, 10 to 15 minutes. Stir in shrimp and parsley. Cover and cook one minute. Serves 6.

TRIFLE WITH THE DETAILS

BY BRUCE YOUNG

My wife, Margaret, and I like to do things as a team, and when that doesn't work, we compete. Each of us specializes in certain desserts. One of my specialties is brownie pudding cake. I've made it with and without recipes, on at least two continents. It has turned out different every time. One of Margaret's specialties is trifle, a traditional English dessert—which actually comes from *my* side of the family.

We both have English ancestry, among various other strains. On my side, one of the English lines made a detour through Australia on its way to Utah. Trifle is also associated with New Zealand, where my father served a mission. In fact, when I asked Margaret how she came up with her recipe for trifle, she said, "I don't remember. Lots of places. I got some of it from your dad." Maybe that's one reason she likes to use slices of kiwi in her version of trifle, or maybe the kiwi just helps complete the color combination.

My mother, Ruth W. Young, thinks of trifle in connection with her grandmother Caroline Annie Merchant Wilson, who was born of English parents in Australia in 1841. Caroline recorded that "in 1854 part of the family were converted to the Mormon church and in 1855 Mother and six children sailed from Sydney on board the American Ship *Julia Ann*." Caroline's father didn't come, supposedly because the captain wouldn't allow him to smoke his pipe on the wooden ship. When the pipe was snatched from his mouth and thrown overboard by the captain before departure, Caroline's father went back to shore. The portion of the family that stayed on board arrived in America about two and a half months later and lived in San Bernardino until 1857, when they moved to Utah. Caroline married Thomas Henry Wilson in 1859 and lived in Payson, Utah, until her death in 1919.

Another story, possibly apocryphal (like the one about the pipe), indicates that when Thomas Henry Wilson was considering taking a second wife, Caroline invited the woman to dinner. In my mother's words: "She prepared a fine meal, which she served to the family and guest without sitting down with them. When she served dessert she got the milk pail and egg basket and addressed the lady under consideration. She is supposed to have said, 'It will be nice when you marry Mr. Wilson. Then I can sit down at the table and be waited on as you serve the meals you have prepared. And you can milk the cow and gather the eggs, and do the other chores.' Needless to say, Mr. Wilson never took a second wife." Somehow I don't think trifle was on the menu at that dinner.

We don't know, in fact, whether Caroline was a trifle maker, though the dish was popular in Australia as well as England. My mother began making it mainly because my father's mission in New Zealand had made him a lover of trifle. He worked among the Maori, but enjoyed the trifle that the English settlers had introduced to New Zealand, which was popular among the Maori as well. I think Margaret acquired her interest in trifle partly from the times my mother made it. But Margaret soon made the dessert her own, giving her own distinctive twist to the recipe.

We have a large bowl we make trifle in—a trifle bowl, in fact, though we didn't know at first that that was what it was. It is a clear glass cylindrical container standing on a stem with a base. The stem is about five or six inches high; the container itself is about eight inches deep and about a foot in diameter. We always feel it's a bit of a shame to eat the trifle because it looks so good. Looking at the trifle bowl from the side, you can see the layers of cake, Jello, pudding, and whipped cream—and especially the colorful bits of fruit.

As I noted, we didn't know it was a trifle bowl at first. We got it as a wedding present, and when

Margaret saw it, she thought of fish. We didn't actually keep fish in it for long periods. But whenever the water in our fish bowl needed changing, Margaret put the fish and the old water temporarily in the trifle bowl. When we found out what it was really for, Margaret cleaned the bowl very thoroughly before using it for trifle. (A special note to those we've fed trifle to: the bowl hasn't been used for fish for years. And none of you have gotten sick, have you? Have you?)

When we eat trifle, I spend most of my energy simply enjoying it, for it is truly one of the world's great desserts. But I sometimes reminisce a bit, too. I think of my great-great-grandfather Merchant's pipe; the goldfish who used to spend short periods in the trifle bowl; my father's mission among the Maori of New Zealand. And I think of my great-grandmother Caroline Annie Merchant Wilson. Though I never met her, I can picture her—tall, much taller than her husband, wearing a dark dress and a long, white apron. Her descendants report her to have been a loving mother and grandmother. She never set foot in England, but she passed on English ways and English loves. And she seems to have passed on an inclination for trifle.

Margaret Blair Young's Trifle

*Break or cut an angel food cake into smallish pieces, bite-sized or a bit larger, and line the bottom of a large bowl with the pieces. A trifle bowl is nice, but any bowl will do. (We don't recommend fish bowls, though.) Though we prefer angel food cake, any white cake will do in a pinch.

*Dissolve one small package (3 ounces) Jello (any fruit flavor) in 2 cups hot water. Pour hot liquid over the cake.

*Add a layer of vanilla custard or pudding. (Bird's Pudding Powder is popular among the English, but we use whatever we find in the local supermarket. If using Jello pudding, use a large box.)

*Over the custard or pudding, add a layer of fruit. Any fruit will do, including canned or frozen, but fresh fruit is best. Margaret's favorites include berries (strawberries, raspberries, blackberries, boysenberries) and banana and kiwi slices. Other possibilities include grapes and pineapple. The main thing is to be creative and to make both the taste and the color tantalizing.

*Over the fruit, add a layer of whipped cream.

*If a large enough bowl is used, the layers— cake, Jello, custard or pudding, fruit, and whipped cream—can be repeated as many as four times, or until the bowl is full.

Traditional trifle uses wine or sherry, but the Mormon version uses fruit juice or Jello instead. Many other variations in the ingredients are possible.

CONFESSIONS OF
A WEASEL

By Lael Littke

It was one of those tidbits of wisdom that appear on the Internet now and then: "Eagles may soar, but weasels aren't sucked into jet engines."

I laughed because I'd just been asked to provide a gourmet main dish to a party, and as usual I had weaseled out. "I don't do gourmet," I told the hostess. "But I'll bring a salad that will be on the positive side of presentable."

She didn't object. She'd probably heard of my Earthquake Enchiladas (all broken up) and my Flooding Flan (it isn't supposed to spread out all over the plate).

But salads are easy. You don't run the risk of a

soufflé transmuting into a crepe because you drop a can of cat food on the stove while it's baking. Or a sauce that curdles just because you walk past it.

I've tried the fancy stuff. I used to believe my friends who would suggest some elegant dish with the promise, "I've got a never-fail recipe you can try."

They erased the "never-fail" part after I'd tried it.

My Boeuf au Fromage went back to France. My Chocolate Decadence with Creme Anglaise and Raspberry Puree putrefied. Even my Firehouse Chowder burned down.

Let the soaring eagles of the kitchen do those dishes and take their chances with the jet engines. I'm staying down here with the weasels. My Salad de Supermarket is pretty nutritious, and absolutely no-fail unless you drench it with too much dressing. Just buy one of those nifty packages of prewashed baby lettuces and a jar of chilled citrus pieces from the produce department (expensive, but worth it). Put them together and toss with a raspberry vinaigrette dressing. M-m-m, good!

I do have one recipe that I make when I can't avoid company. It was given to me by an English lad who stayed with us for a while and got desperate for something edible. I call it simply "Curried Beef" because if I gave it a fancy name I'd have to compete with the eagles.

CURRIED BEEF

1 pound or more of beef, either stew meat or
    round steak cut into bite-sized chunks
1 small onion, chopped
1 small apple, chopped
4 or 5 mushrooms, sliced
2 cloves garlic (or to taste), minced
Vegetable oil
¼ teaspoon turmeric (optional)
½ teaspoon dry mustard
¼ teaspoon pepper
1 tablespoon flour (you may need more)
1 cup stock (I use a teaspoon of beef bouillon dis-
    solved in 1 cup water)
1 teaspoon curry powder (at least)
Pinches of dried parsley, sage, thyme (optional)
¼ cup raisins
½ banana, mashed

Sauté beef until well browned. Set aside. Sauté onion, apple, mushrooms, and garlic in small amount of oil. When tender, add turmeric (if desired), mustard, pepper, and flour, stirring with the other sautéed ingredients and adding more oil, if needed, to make a paste. When paste is hot and bubbly, add stock, curry powder, other spices if desired, and raisins, stirring to make a smooth sauce. Add meat. Heat gently until thick. Add mashed banana 10 minutes before serving.

Can be served with couscous for a Moroccan-type meal, or with plain rice. Even with noodles, if that's what you do best. Serves 6 to 8.

STONE SOUP
FOR THE SOUL

BY MARY LYTHGOE BRADFORD

One cold March day, we heard in Relief Society that the husband of one of our number was ill with kidney stones. The brother assured his wife that his kidney stones were as agonizing as the pains of childbirth. We asked ourselves how he could possibly know, but our compassionate natures won out. We would alleviate the pain of mankind. My friend Belle and I went into action. Reasoning that he would need both nourishment and comfort, we chose a wholesome soup recipe another friend had contributed to my file.

Belle and I decided to call our concoction a modern version of "Stone Soup," after a favorite children's folktale in which two destitute French soldiers, returning from the war, stop at a village to ask for room and board for the night. Fearful villagers refuse them, hiding their viands and claiming deprivation. Finally the soldiers announce that if the villagers will lend them a pot, they will make a wonderful soup. As the villagers gather to watch, the soldiers ask for smooth stones to drop into boiling water. "Wouldn't it be grand if we had a carrot or two to add?" they muse, and the villagers add not only carrots but potatoes, then meat—until an entire feast "miraculously" appears. *Our* version of Stone Soup would miraculously dissolve kidney stones and feed three families while it was at it.

We vowed to use only the best ingredients, including fresh vegetables—no canned stuff, except for canned beef stock. Nowadays cooks have really good electric choppers and shredders that cut preparation time to mere minutes. I couldn't even contribute an archaic food processor. Armed only with a large pot, a cutting board, a hand shredder, and some knives, we set to work. We spent hours peeling, scraping, and chopping. The beets were our undoing. We discovered afterwards that had we cooked them first, we could have shucked the peelings easily. But we conscientiously peeled the beets—and our knuckles. We excused ourselves by declaring, "What good is Stone Soup without blood, sweat, and tears?"

As we worked, we relived some of the struggles we had survived with the help of the Relief Society. For us, this really was a society that believed in giving relief, and we never hesitated to call in the sisters when we needed relief of any kind. This mosaic of a soup, this artist's rendition of culinary comfort, would stand as a testament of Relief Society's message in concrete form. (I suppose *concrete* is not the right word, since we hoped the soup would keep Kent's innards from turning to concrete.)

As we clumsily prepared our offering, we celebrated our enterprising, compassionate sisters. We paid tribute to Jill, who had kept her tiny house full of children and grandchildren all the while she was composing poetry and devising imaginative ways to teach a Down's syndrome daughter. We mentioned Deanne, who, from her post as a clerk in the neighborhood baby store, arranged to deliver slightly damaged but good strollers, cribs, and clothes to our struggling children who were facing parenthood. We thought of Pam, who, after the tragic death of a child, went back to school and became a creative special education teacher. We honored Margo, who founded a "Thursday Lunch" whereby she delivered box lunches to neighborhood businesses, and to us when we were too weak to cook. We honored Ruth, who, widowed too soon, went to school and became an art historian so she could offer classes in her home and arrange tours to the world's great museums. Many of us gained our love of art through her. We remembered Charlotte, owner of the soup recipe we were using. She was a maker of handmade dolls and heavenly ice cream, both of which she sold for a pittance. The year my daughter left for a mission, I purchased a doll "stand-in" for her. It still sits in my living room waiting for visits from the grandchildren. These women fed us spiritually, emotionally, and physically.

The soup became a stew of good memories. We thought of all the other "soups" that had saved us—the casseroles and kindnesses, the box lunches and buggies, the ice cream and ideas. Our Stone Soup became an offering on the altar of sisterly relief and love. And, sure enough, our friend's kidney stones disappeared and to this day have not reappeared.

Charlotte's Stone Soup for the Soul

In a large kettle, combine:

2 cups finely chopped carrots
4 cups finely chopped onions
4 cups finely chopped celery
4 cups finely chopped parsnips

Add enough water to cover. Bring to a boil; reduce heat and simmer for twenty minutes. Then add:

4 cups chopped, cooked beets (cook first, then slice off peelings, or used canned beets)
4 tablespoons butter
2 quarts beef stock
4 cups shredded cabbage
4 cups tomato pulp (preferably whole canned tomatoes, pureed)
3 tablespoons vinegar

Simmer for 15 minutes. Serve with a blob of sour cream. Serves 20.

DADDY'S FOOD

BY LINDA HOFFMAN KIMBALL

When I was a child, some of the things my dad ate gave me the creeps. He was a big Chicagoan of German extraction, fond of sausages and potatoes. That wouldn't have been so bad. I like sausages and potatoes too. But those other things! I'd come home from playing on a Saturday to a kitchen redolent of his huge, boiling batch of sauerkraut. Hard to invite your buddies in when the whole house smells like it's going to explode. And once in a while he'd take to making split pea soup. Why would anyone want to make food that smelled and looked so . . . organic? But the worst, the absolute worst, were the clear glass jars of pickled pig's feet. Pink. Nude. Gelatinous. Simply horrific.

My dad also liked vinegar. Lots of it. Especially as a salad dressing. Unfortunately, he also erupted into violent coughing spasms whenever he ate it. This happened at

45

nearly every meal. My two sisters and my mom and I grew used to Daddy seizing up and shaking the bench of the dining nook with his racking coughs. We would just chat and continue eating, quite ignoring him until he regained his composure. I remember how alarmed my little friend Kris Johnson was when Daddy launched into his cataclysmic vinegar seizure one night when she had dinner with us. There was a look of panic on her face that said simultaneously, "What's wrong with this man?" and, "Why aren't the rest of you doing anything about it?"

My mom, who prepared most meals, got a day off on Sunday, when Daddy would fix a roast or poultry of some sort. These meals were not scary occasions in any way. They were delicious. In those days, before *cholesterol* became a household word, my sisters and I used to compete for "the crispy stuff"—the glistening, amber skin of the turkey or chicken. Daddy's apple-and-sausage stuffing for turkey was then and continues to be one of my all-time favorite foods. Also, though the name embarrassed me, I really liked one particular pork meal my dad made—smoked butt.

Daddy had some favorite sayings he would trot out at the dinner table. If I complained about fat on my meat portion, he would predictably say, "You need that to grease the chutes." I wasn't sure what that meant, but he said it with such authority that I gobbled up whatever was on my plate. He had another gem for baked potatoes. It was important to eat potato skins, he consistently told his three daughters, because "it'll put hair on your chest." Usually, when a meal was over, he had some little kindness for my mom: "Real good, Sooz," or something like that. It was always interesting to me that he called my mom "Sooz." Her name was Mary. It might have made sense as a nickname for my sister Susan, but no, for some private reason, my mother was "Sooz" to him.

Favorite sayings of a different sort got Daddy into hot water once, but I loved him for it. I stayed home sick from school one winter day with a queasy stomach. When my dad got home from work that night, he came into my room. There I lay, propped up with pillows and books to beat my boredom.

"Here's a little surprise for you," he said.

He held out a bag full of colorful Valentine candy hearts, the kind with little sayings on them: "Luv You," "Cool Kid," "Dig It."

I was thrilled. My mom was furious. I remember overhearing some heated exchange about the appropriateness of giving a whole bag of candy to a little girl who hadn't been able to keep a thing down all day. I knew even at nine years old that he had given me something much more nourishing than candy that day.

My dad died in 1973, when I was twenty. How can it possibly be so long ago? I think of him every time I eat potato skins or make his stuffing or put vinegar on my salad or indulge in one of my now favorite soups— split pea. And there have been occasions in grocery stores when I have been caught off guard and found myself crying in front of glass jars of pink, gelatinous, pickled pig's feet.

Luv You, Daddy.

AL HOFFMAN'S APPLE-SAUSAGE STUFFING

1 pound pork sausage

¾ cup butter or margarine

¾ cup chopped onion

1½ cups chopped celery

8 cups cheap, soft, white bread, torn into 1½-inch
    pieces

1 teaspoon salt

1 teaspoon poultry seasoning

¾ teaspoon ground sage

¾ teaspoon ground thyme

½ teaspoon black pepper

3 apples (Granny Smith are great), cored, peeled,
    and cut into 1-inch chunks

Brown pork sausage. Remove sausage from drippings and set aside.

Melt butter or margarine in pan with sausage drippings. Add onion and celery and stir until tender.

In a large mixing bowl, put about 2½ cups of the torn bread. Pour in the butter and vegetables. Mix until damp. Add spices, sausage, apples, and remaining bread. Mix, preferably by hand, until well incorporated. Stuff in poultry for roasting or bake separately in a covered dish at 325 degrees F. for 30 minutes.

SPLIT PEA SOUP

2 cups dried split peas
2 quarts water
1 pound ham chunks
1 cup finely chopped celery
1 medium onion, finely chopped (about ½ cup)
1 bay leaf
¼ teaspoon pepper

Heat peas and water to boiling; boil gently for 2 minutes. Remove from heat. Allow to stand, covered, for 1 hour.

Add remaining ingredients. Simmer 2½ to 3 hours until peas are soft. Thin with milk or water if desired. Season with salt or more pepper to taste. Serves 6 (1 cup each).

Ninja Pork Chops

By David Dollahite

I was raised in a fairly devout Episcopalian home. I can't say that I ever noticed a relationship between our religion and food, except, of course, for the consecrated wafers and wine at Holy Communion. I do know that high church Episcopalian belief does *not* include the practice of food storage. We were squarely in the middle class, but my mother aspired to the lifestyle of the affluent Episcopalian gentility. Thus, she was not especially prone to practice frugality in general, nor food frugality in particular. We ate out often, were the first in our circle to own a microwave, and ate a lot of TV dinners.

I began my Mormon culinary journey in paradise, enjoying the delectable cooking of Sister LoDonna Leininger. Ray and LoDonna Leininger took their food almost as seriously as their missionary responsibilities, and I was the happy beneficiary of both. Therefore, at the same time I was feasting on the Word, I also supped many times at the Leininger's table before missionary lessons, home evenings, and firesides held at their home. The food was plentiful, filling, and sweet. In a word, celestial.

For years following, nearly every meal was only a shadow of the gastronomical glory I had experienced in my new-convert primeval paradise. I am ashamed to say that in my first few years of marriage I often spoke wistfully to my wife, Mary, about my days in culinary heaven. Thankfully, she took all this in good humor. Mary is blessed with a cheerful confidence and a solid and nurturing family with pioneer heritage *all the way back, on both sides,* and is practically perfect in every way. She is also perfectly practical in every way, and sometimes Mary's pioneer frugality and my unrealistic culinary expectations have come into conflict. This occurred most sharply during what I call the "Ninja Pork Chops Era."

I sometimes tease Mary that she and her family live by the Articles of Frugality, which include: "We believe that all things can be saved, by obedience to the principles of frugality," "We believe in the gifts of coupons, yard sales, hand-me-downs, patches, Deseret Industries, and so forth," "If there is anything old, or used, or broken-but-repair-worthy, we seek to keep these things."

All this was fine with me when it came to things like hanging on to the old car a few more years, or using a thirty-year-old crib—given us by a fellow graduate student—through four children. But when it came to *food frugality,* I confess I had a harder time. Though I tried to get a practical testimony of this principle, it did not come quickly or easily—it came can upon can, pork chop upon pork chop.

In 1989 we had been married for nearly six years, living on the salary of a new assistant professor and paying off large student loans. One day during one of our visits to Utah, Mary's mother emerged from the food-storage area in her basement with numerous huge cans of freeze-dried pork chops. Mary was thrilled with our share of the bounty: twelve #5 size cans, to be exact. This was no problem for me, until I was told that the pork chops were originally packaged for the U.S. Army by the Oscar Meyer company in the early 1960s, and that these particular cans had been rejected by the Army as not conforming to their specifications. My in-laws' bishop, who happened to work for Oscar Meyer, had made the rejected food available to his ward, and Mary's frugal parents had purchased a good many cans for food storage at twenty-five cents a can.

I wondered: If the Army, not exactly known for its great food, didn't want them in the first place, why did we have to eat them a quarter of a century later? I thought I remembered hearing something about the importance of rotation in food storage, and twenty-five years seemed like a long rotation cycle. I wondered aloud whether fossilized, reconstituted, freeze-dried trichinosis was as deadly as it sounded. Mary calmly called the State Agricultural Agent and found out that twenty-five-year-old freeze-dried pork chops were probably safe, though the agent offered no such assurance about their nutritional value, except as roughage.

Each freeze-dried pork chop was about the size of a 3½-inch computer disk and the consistency and appearance of old, sturdy cardboard. Because of how they looked, their military origin, the martial-artsy sound of "chops," and the fact that I was sure they would be silent killers, I referred to them as "Ninja Pork Chops." I suggested to Mary that, rather than eat them, we should continue to store them so that when the last days came and marauding food-storage robbers showed up at our home to plunder our wheat and powdered milk, we could just hand these cans out to buy them off. Or, if really pressed, we could break out the chops from their cans, sharpen them, and use them like those sharp-pointed metal weapons that ninja assassins flick at their victims. I told Mary it was my opinion that the second approach would actually be the more Christian thing to do.

Regardless, since my testimony of food frugality was not yet strong, I did not believe I was being unfaithful to my religion when I told Mary that I *would not* eat twenty-five-year-old Army Surplus pork chops, nor would I allow my children to do so—devoted husband and moderately frugality-friendly guy though I was. Mary took my protest in stride and served them up anyway. She soaked them overnight to rehydrate them, let them simmer for several hours, and then made a casserole with mushroom soup and rice—the meat added "for flavor."

Despite my valiant and, I believed, legitimate protests, I knew I had to eat those chops in order to prove to my in-laws, my wife, and my sixth-generation Mormon children that, although I was just a recent convert from California, I too could endure hardship for my faith. We then had a period of three or four months when, about once a week, we ate twenty-five-year-old pork chops for dinner.

This became a time in our marriage when mealtime meant much more to me than just coming home to eat, drink, and see Mary. I thought of those long months as my personal trek toward True Pioneer Mormonism. Mary's pioneer frugality not only gave us many great-tasting, inexpensive meals during a time of financial stress but turned hard times into defining lessons. It even taught me several gospel principles. The importance of the blessing over the food took on new meaning for me. I obtained a much better gut-level sense of how "dem dry bones" can be made to return to life after such a long time. And I saw that Mary had unwittingly acted in the pattern of the Prophet Joseph himself, by taking something very old and translating it for use by another generation.

After all of this, however, I have a confession: Mary's Ninja Pork Chop Casserole actually tasted pretty good. In fact, it tasted *really* good, and I almost began to look forward to it. Of course, I did not dare tell Mary this, since I had no idea what else might still be lingering in my in-laws' food storage. And now that our food budget allows Mary a little more freedom, our evening meals are a lot like those I remember from my early days in Mormon mealtime paradise. Mary's cooking is absolutely heavenly—in a down-to-earth, frugal-Mormon sort of way.

MARY'S NINJA PORK CHOP CASSEROLE

(An Old Family Recipe)

8 to 12 pork chops

2 cups uncooked white rice

2 teaspoons salt

2 cans cream of mushroom soup

2 tablespoons dried parsley flakes

2 teaspoons sage

1. Place pork chops (preferably Oscar Meyer, U.S. Army Issue, freeze-dried, circa 1962) in pan of water to rehydrate for 24 hours. (Place plate weighted with soup cans on top of chops to keep them from floating.)

2. Simmer for 3 to 4 hours or until pliable. (In an emergency, or a time of frugality-weakness, substitute fresh medallion pork chops and skip steps 1 and 2.)

3. Spread uncooked rice in the bottom of a 9 x 13-inch baking dish. Sprinkle with salt. Add 4½ cups water. Arrange chops on rice. Spoon undiluted cream of mushroom soup over chops and rice. Sprinkle with parsley and sage.

4. Bake in 325 degree F. oven for 1 hour.

LoDonna's Cheese and Canadian Bacon Brunch Casserole

(Served at a reception following David's baptism)

4 or 5 slices buttered French bread
2 cups grated cheddar cheese
6 eggs
1 teaspoon dry mustard
3 cups milk
Salt and pepper to taste
1 pound Canadian bacon or ham pieces

Break buttered French bread into bite-sized pieces into greased 9 x 13-inch baking dish. Sprinkle the grated cheese over the bread. In a medium-sized bowl, beat the eggs, then add the mustard, milk, and salt and pepper to taste (about ½ teaspoon salt and ⅛ teaspoon pepper). Pour over bread in baking dish. Cover with foil and refrigerate overnight.

The following morning, layer the top with bite-sized pieces of Canadian bacon or ham, cover with foil, and bake in a 250 degree F. oven for 2 hours. (If you're in more of a hurry in the morning, bake at 350 degrees F. for 20 minutes covered with foil and 20 more minutes uncovered.) Casserole is done when you can take a knife and slice it into squares for serving. Serves 10 to 12.

FAITH, REFRESHMENTS, AND BAPTISM

BY NANCY HARWARD

When I reached the age of accountability in Southern California in the early '60s, our monthly baptismal services were rather impersonal affairs. At mine, dozens—possibly hundreds—of white-clad eight-year-olds filled the chapel of the stake center. Unfamiliar adults from other wards appeared at the pulpit to teach us about making covenants and receiving the Holy Ghost, and then we fidgeted to quiet organ music as we waited to be called to the font, row by row, as directed.

To my young eyes, the font room appeared as busy as a packing house. Fascinated, I watched apple-cheeked children move steadily along a conveyor that washed them, dried them, stamped them full-fledged members, and shipped them out as a new crop came in. Suddenly recognizing a friend from another ward, I called a greeting across the crowded room—and was amazed that my mother would reprimand me for being irreverent amid so much bustle. The only other twinge in my general elation was concern that the blue tag in my otherwise pure white clothing might nullify the whole experience.

By the time my children were old enough to be baptized, I had moved to the opposite coast. In Delaware, where it takes half a day to drive from one end of the stake to the other, we try to avoid traveling beyond our own ward meetinghouses for anything but the most essential stake activities. Baptisms, therefore, are usually scheduled as needed by individual wards rather than monthly by the stake. Frequently, bishops allow families to plan their own services. These intimate gatherings are more memorable than the mass productions of more densely populated stakes. Only at a family-run affair would you draw open the doors of the font before an eager audience and discover that no one had remembered to fill it. Only at a service where younger siblings said the prayers would you hear a five-year-old boy thank the Lord that his sister had turned eight, so that she could be baptized into the Cub Scouts.

What really distinguishes these family baptisms, however, is the food. In our ward, a baptism is almost as lavish as a wedding reception, especially if it has been scheduled for those Sunday afternoon hours between the last sacrament meeting and the early evening fire-side. Knowing that everyone will be famished and won't have time to go home for dinner, we come prepared. Tray after heaping tray, the goodies are lined up along the counter in the kitchen (or rather the "Serving Area," for we never "cook" there): chips and dips, cheese and crackers, fruit and veggie platters for the women who keep teaching those "heart healthy" cooking classes at homemaking meeting, cookies, punch, maybe some Rice Krispie treats, and brownies—always brownies.

Most people resort to mixes, but we always make our brownies from scratch, using the recipe that my husband, Michael, got from a former missionary companion. I usually make them plain, but if Michael makes them, he's likely to stir in some peanut butter or coconut or something we can't quite identify. The kids like them better plain.

Stacey Engebretsen makes her brownies from scratch too, with Belgian chocolate left over from her holiday truffle business. She cuts them into tiny, perfect squares, dusting them lightly with powdered sugar. Children pass them by, eyeing the gooey three-inchers on the next plate, and the more discriminating among us are grateful for Stacey's foresight.

Carmen Jones puts walnuts in her brownies; Karin Sumpter's have marshmallow creme. Pat Hollingshaus brings frosted ones, with a thin layer of green mint filling. They disappear quickly.

Sister Robertson's recipe calls for mashed banana instead of shortening, carob instead of cocoa. "They're very low in fat," she explains. Later I see many of Sister Robertson's brownies on abandoned plates, next to strawberry stems and spreading clumps of spinach dip.

Last summer, we held a Sunday evening baptism for the child of a "less-active" ward member. My sister-in-law Pat was the mother's visiting teacher. She had made most of the arrangements and was anxious to see that the family had a positive experience. Michael and I helped her mix punch and ready a couple of trays of brownies in the serving area while the font finished filling; then we took our seats. Minutes before the service began, the family members arrived—fifty-three of them! Grandparents, aunts, uncles, cousins, ex-husbands, stepchildren, everybody.

"There isn't enough food," Pat hissed at Michael from the piano bench as he directed the opening hymn. "What are we going to do?"

When the song was over, my husband didn't return to his seat (it had been taken anyway), but walked to the back and quietly slipped out the door. Knowing he couldn't make the forty-five-minute round trip home and back before the closing prayer, I wondered where he was going to get more food, but had faith that somehow, he and the Lord would provide.

A while later, Pat sneaked out of the baptism to cut the brownies into smaller portions. With grateful relief, she discovered that the serving area was already spread with cold-cut platters, baskets of chips, and an assortment of dips from the deli section of the local Acme.

Afterward, the brownies were gone, but there were

enough cold cuts to divide up and take home. "What a beautiful service," I heard someone comment on the way out. "We have truly been filled."

More recently, my eight-year-old and I had to miss a friend's Saturday afternoon baptism because of an appointment we couldn't change. When we returned home, the house was empty. It was time to fix dinner.

"Where is everybody?" my daughter wondered.

"I guess they're still at the baptism."

"Can we go?" she asked, her eyes suddenly eager.

"Why bother?" I said, pouring leftover spaghetti sauce into a pot. "It was supposed to start an hour ago, so even if we left right now, I'm sure it would be over by the time we got to the church."

"Can we go anyway?" she begged. "Please?"

"Why do you want to go to a baptism that's already over?"

"Because," she replied, "there might still be some refreshments!"

Elder Hansen's Brownies

1 cup margarine
4 ounces semisweet chocolate pieces
2 cups sugar
4 eggs
1½ cups flour
1 teaspoon baking powder
¾ teaspoon salt

Preheat oven to 350 degrees F. In a large saucepan, slowly heat the margarine with the chocolate, stirring until melted and smooth. Combine melted mixture with sugar. Add eggs one at a time, mixing well after each. Stir in flour, baking powder, and salt. Pour into a greased 9 x 13-inch pan and bake for 35 to 40 minutes, or until a toothpick inserted in center comes out clean. Cool for 20 minutes, then cut into squares. Makes about 24.

Pat's Layered Mint Brownies

First layer:
¼ cup margarine
1 cup sugar
6 tablespoons cocoa
1 egg
1 cup flour
1 teaspoon baking powder
½ cup evaporated milk

Preheat oven to 350 degrees F. Combine margarine, sugar, and cocoa. Stir in egg. Combine flour with baking powder and add to creamed mixture alternately with evaporated milk, stirring until blended. Pour into a greased 9 x 13-inch pan and bake 10 minutes. Cool.

Second layer:

2 cups powdered sugar

¼ cup margarine

¼ teaspoon peppermint extract

2 drops green food coloring

1 to 2 tablespoons evaporated milk

Cream powdered sugar and margarine. Add peppermint, coloring, and 1 tablespoon evaporated milk. Beat until smooth, adding more milk if needed to reach spreading consistency. Spread over first layer and allow to set.

Third layer:

6 tablespoons margarine

1 cup chocolate chips

Melt margarine and chocolate chips together, stirring until smooth. Cool. Spread over second layer. Chill in refrigerator until chocolate layer sets. Cut into 1½-inch squares. Makes about 48.

An Anglophile Reflects on The Yorkshire Pudding

By Richard H. Cracroft

You need to understand a few things before you partake of The Yorkshire Pudding: It is a dish that must be eaten with an attitude—of reverence for the hearty, beef-eating people from which the dish arose in the dawn of (London) history; of respect for British seafaring history; of awe, by one who savors at once the rich, dripping-permeated pudding and the millennium it has taken to evolve not only the perfect pudding, but the perfect Yorkshire-Pudding-Eater.

I am such a Pudding-Eater. I modestly profess to bring to the table at which the steaming Yorkshire presides that complex combination of history and heritage, genetics and appetite, gratitude and reverence that produces, after generations, the American, Australian, Argentine, Canadian, Englishman, New Zealander, Scot, or South African who has the temperament, taste, breeding—and the marbled beef—to be the *bona fide* Yorkshire-Pudding-Eater.

Again, I am such a Being: born of goodly first-generation-out-of-England parents, I have been carefully steeped in English history and tradition, rocked to sleep to British lullabies, and read to from British nursery rhymes. I have eaten off Sunday-best bone china brought from "the old country," and poured my Worcestershire or mint sauce in rooms displaying the portraits of King George VI and Elizabeth II. My earliest recorded ancestor, Rothgar, fought at the Battle of Hastings, and I, Richard, grew up "God-blessing-America" in one breath and "God-saving-the-King" in the next. And, with Grandma White, singing with gusto that "Britons"—at that time under *Luftwaffe* attack—"ne-vah, ne-vah, nevah will be slaves!"

I grew up knowing I was a Mormon boy, a Utahn, an American, and, woven through all those identities, a proud grandson of Grandmother England. And you may not forget this singular fact (as I was never allowed to): my grandmother's first cousin was the favorite lady-in-waiting of Queen Victoria herself. I was born to be a Yorkshire-Pudding-Eater *par excellence*.

American my family is, but, thanks to my mother and my likewise born-of-goodly-British-parents father, we ate as well as spoke English in our home. Rather, we ate Mormon Reconstituted English. This meant loyalty to a few simple but irrational dietary facts:

1. People who drank coffee were un-British, un-American, and unsalvageable; they were low class (always spoken by my mother *sotto voce,* like when she said "Democrat" or "apostate"). They were even lower than those who served casseroles (aargh), and lower still than those who served pumpkin pie (yuck). Thus I was seventeen before I tasted (and loved) either, and my mother, outraged on learning that my girlfriend's family had served both casserole and pumpkin pie (no coffee, thank heaven), urged me to look "among our kind" for worthier companions.

2. Although it carried no coffee-onus because it was the drink of kings, green tea was strictly forbidden in our Mormon home—except as a prescribed medicament for a serious ailment (defined as anything from hangnail to bad hair day to terminal cancer). As medicine, tea (unlike coffee) was clearly approved by the Lord. Produced in the Queen's colonies, tea was the drink of kings, who were, after all, God's appointees. When I was served a cup of tea and piece of buttered toast in bed, I knew (oh joy!) I was deemed too sick to go to school that day.

3. Finally, certain approved English dishes (Grandma's recipes) were served on Sundays and at family gatherings by my genius-in-the-kitchen but self-effacing mother, who was all atremble in fearful anticipation of our (always laudatory) verdicts. We did not

merely eat these English dishes, we *partook* with a certain sacramental reverence for the storied nation and people with which we were, at that moment, gastronomically and spiritually one.

These foods remained unchanged across the generations of true bloods: fruitcake wrapped in mysteriously "soaked" towels (we were told "never you mind" when we asked about the "soak") and aged for six weeks, figgy pudding, hot-cross buns, heavenly dinner rolls, finnan haddie (on Christmas morning only), leg of lamb, salmon baked in a towel, and (pause for trumpet flourish) the mother dish, the Dish of Dishes, the dish of St. George, the Dragon, the beef-eating Englishman, and the Spiritually British in every nation: *The Yorkshire Pudding.*

There is nothing more delicious than The Yorkshire Pudding. Scholars are unanimous: crediting our First Parents with intelligence and good taste, they recently announced that it was The Yorkshire Pudding, not an apple, that brought down Adam and Eve. Think about it: which of God's creations, having eaten the heavenly Yorkshire at their premortal celestial hearths, and having retained the experience in genetic memory, would have given up immortality for a mere *apple?* Following this recent discovery about the Yorkshire's Edenic role, other inspired scholars have suggested the logical destiny of the dish. You may have read it here first: the Resurrection will rouse the Dead, and the Coming Forth will commence when the Dead, breaking off the bonds of death and the shackles of hell, wake up and smell the heavenly, the eternal, the celestial aroma of the favorite dish of the triumphant King Himself: The Yorkshire Pudding.

THE YORKSHIRE PUDDING

Bake a 4- to 5-pound beef roast (rump is good) at 350 degrees F. for about 2½ hours, until nicely browned.

When roast is done, remove from roasting pan and keep warm.

To the roast drippings in roasting pan, add 1 cup water and 1 teaspoon salt. Heat to boiling in 400 degree F. oven.

Prepare the pudding ingredients:

2 cups flour

1 teaspoon salt

2 cups milk

4 eggs

1 teaspoon baking powder

Stir flour and salt together in a medium bowl. Combine milk and eggs; stir into dry ingredients. Add baking powder; stir again.

Into the boiling roast drippings in roasting pan, quickly pour pudding mixture. DO NOT STIR.

Place in 400 degree F. oven. Bake without opening oven for ½ hour. Tread lightly. Remove from oven and serve immediately. Makes 6 richly brown, succulent servings, plus smaller second helpings.

Sing "God Save the Queen."

My Sister's Banquet

By Judy Dushku

My sister Trish always told people that she was a Mormon, but Mormons called her "inactive." Aside from frequent reports she got from me or my children about this or that member, this new calling or that talk given, her contact with the Church was negligible. But year after year she welcomed ever-changing sets of home and visiting teachers who approached her big home in Brookline, Massachusetts, with a mix of curiosity and confusion.

To her New England neighbors Trish was something of an exotic. She played Mormon hymns on the piano and sang them to whomever. She told stories of her cowboy daddy from Idaho. But otherwise she seemed part of the old Yankee culture that defined the neighborhood of big, old homes with carriage houses out back and servant entrances and kitchen stairs inside. She was happy there, an "immigrant" from another life that began in the Snake River Valley. Trish, like her tradition-bound neighbors, made Yorkshire Pudding and crown rib roast, served fruitcake with hard sauce, and for everyday made corned beef and cabbage. Brookline town meetings were held in the living room, the blue willow stoneware was kept in the kitchen, and the Limoges dessert plates were stacked in the pantry.

Trish was outrageously blunt and intrusive in a manner that surprised people initially and later made them glad and tied them to her in deep and urgent ways. She loved to visit and be visited. She actually set up a mini-visiting teaching program in her neighborhood, assigning herself and others to tend to those who were ill or depressed or grieving. They took in food, visited hospitals, drove each other to airports, housed relatives for each other's weddings. She kept track of folks' ups and downs, and responded with vigor to celebrate or to mourn. People sent her monogrammed cards thanking her for "being with me when I needed it most."

Although Trish had suffered from a serious liver disease for years, it was still a shock when we were told in the summer of 1990 that she had liver cancer and could be expected to live for only a month. With all our experience in hospitals and caring for her while she was recovering, we were not prepared for this job of helping her die well. We were blessed with exceptional hospice nurses who outlined some basics, and our whole complicated family of stepchildren, nieces and nephews, parents, spouses, ex-husbands, in-laws, and legions of fabulous friends descended on her home in waves for what became two beautiful months of precious time. We sat at Trish's bedside and laughed and cried and sang and snoozed and planned what would be her grand memorial service.

Her neighborhood was peopled with serious musicians in the classical tradition. Why not have this service a memorable musical experience, friends suggested, perhaps with string quartets or even a small orchestra? Despite all their offers for musical masterpieces, Trish was firm that her funeral must have both versions of "Abide with Me," number 2 and number 51 in "the old hymnbook." And, of course, "Lead, Kindly Light." She also wanted my little daughter to sing an old Abolitionist song about Harriet Tubman, but that would be the only music not found in the Mormon hymnbook. After all, Trish insisted, this was to be *her* memorial service, and that necessitated it reflecting her Mormonism.

The program was planned and ready for the printer (except for the date) at least a week before Trish died. We all clung to each moment and prayed for something miraculous, although less and less for her to live longer, since she was shrinking away from not eating. She was so delicate and tiny, hardly able to lift her head. Each of us tried desperately to think of something to comfort her or bring her some small pleasure.

Those last days we became somewhat obsessed with trying to find the right foods for her. We suggested all manner of favorites, but her appetite was waning. She sometimes ate half a mashed and buttered boiled egg, and sometimes some ice cream, but to most of our offerings she smiled an apologetic refusal. It seemed that all her generous friends shared our desire to feed her the perfect food, and wonderful neighbors regaled us with the most exquisite offerings. Honestly, night after night the dining room hosted the "buffet to die for": beautiful salads, hot dishes, soufflés, puddings, cakes, hors d'oeuvres arrived like nothing I had ever seen. These were gourmet offerings. We had to tell some repeaters to stop. We froze things and passed some dishes on to others. It was amazing.

Then Trish stopped eating altogether. She spoke more and more about our grandfather, whom she was sure was waiting. A dear former bishop came to "home teach" her for the last time. Each hour was precious as we watched her say her good-byes to this life. Sometimes she seemed to be living somewhere between us and elsewhere. It was a pure and sweet time.

And then, just days before she died, she perked up when we asked for the hundredth time what she wanted to eat. There was something special, she said apologetically, but it wasn't in the house. But she really had to have it. Would we make the effort? Of course we were eager.

There was a certain woman; could we find her? She was called "the visiting teacher." She made special food, always had. It was important. It was very special. Yes, call the visiting teacher, Trish said in a whisper, and tell her to bring the good food with the tuna and noodles in it. Remember it? she said, almost pleading. It had cream of mushroom soup and cornflakes on top. Could it be re-created? Trish asked urgently that we get this request exactly right. Cheddar on top to make it yellow. . . . You know the kind, she said.

We did. We called Sister Shelley Hammond, and she had it there that night. It was exactly as Trish remembered it, and she ate with pleasure. It was what she needed most to eat before she died. My mother and I took turns feeding it to her.

Tuna Noodle Casserole

1 package (8 ounces) noodles
2 cans (7 ounces each) tuna, well drained
1½ cups sour cream
¾ cup milk
1 can (10 ounces) cream of mushroom soup
1½ teaspoons salt
¼ teaspoon pepper
¼ cup crushed cornflakes
¼ cup grated cheddar cheese
2 tablespoons butter or margarine, melted

Heat oven to 350 degrees F. Cook noodles as directed on package. Return drained noodles to kettle; stir in tuna, sour cream, milk, soup, salt, and pepper. Pour into ungreased 2-quart casserole dish.

Mix cornflakes, cheese, and melted butter or margarine. Sprinkle over casserole. Bake uncovered 35 to 40 minutes or until bubbly.

HOLD YOUR FORK

BY SHERYL CRAGUN DAME

At age nineteen, near the end of the Great War, my grandfather O.B. Harris left the servant-kept home of his uncle in Pittsburgh for the Canadian frontier. It was 1917. An excellent cook, O.B. became a popular hire with the transport companies packing supplies by horse and mule through the mountains between Edmonton, Alberta, and Dawson Creek at the edge of the northwest wilderness. He settled into a tent camp in the Peace River Valley and escorted wealthy prize hunters north to capture enormous fish and horned mountain goats. Then, as the camp became a town, he took his cooking indoors to start a restaurant, where he recreated the standards he had known in Pittsburgh.

He furnished his restaurant in fine hardwoods. Set the tables with silver on crisp, white linens. He chose proper black uniforms for his serving staff and hand-selected his meats from the butcher next door, who hung, smoked, and pickled the cuts to O.B.'s specifications. The menu included baked ham with raisin-cider sauce and roasted lamb with fresh mint sauce. Each morning, in special crockery, O.B. layered navy beans with smoked pork, added mustard powder and dark molasses, and left the mixture to slow-cook all day. During meals he wandered from table to table to swap stories with his guests from throughout the Peace River District—cowboys and expedition guides, homesteaders and gentry.

"Let me tell you how to catch a bear." O.B. liked to share his secrets with friends. On a recent expedition, he said, he'd been attacked by a grizzly. He'd been checking the stew on the fire when he heard it. Still squatting, he turned. As he stood up, the bear swayed closer and closer on its hind legs, swiped its arms and claws, and roared so widely that O.B. could stare past its raw teeth to the back of its throat. To reach his gun would take too long, so O.B. thrust his arm through the bear's wide-open mouth, down its growling throat into its abdomen, then reached deeper and deeper until he felt the bear's tail. He grabbed the tail and pulled back quickly, up through the abdomen and throat, then out the mouth with one deliberate yank groundward. And there you have it: He had turned that bear inside out. Didn't even have to skin it.

Perhaps it was during one of these dinners, in the company of others who relished the West, that O.B.

decided to invite the Duke of Gloucester, then Lieutenant Governor of Alberta Province, to his ranch. O.B. would guide the Duke on a goose shoot in the wetlands there, then serve him an elegant meal in his ranch house. They were no bunch of ruffians, whatever the Duke might think. O.B. arranged for fine linens, silverware, and china. A few local women prepared a fine roast goose, caught the day before, and served it with an herbed cornbread stuffing and an impressive showing of local vegetables. The evening was a near success, said O.B. They had about convinced the Duke they could set a nice table and serve a proper dinner like the rest of them. But just before dessert, as the farmhand's wife cleared the Duke's plate—carefully, from the left side—she noticed his fork on the plate and handed it back to him.

"Hold yer fork, Duke," she said. "Pie comin' up."

At O.B.'s restaurant, the pies included a deep mincemeat. There was also the apple, always served with a generous slice of cheddar cheese. But it is the lemon pie that my family still serves for special guests, the meringue adding a bit of flair to a tangy moment and authentic crust. As O.B. taught us, a little style enhances any adventure.

O.B.'s Lemon Pie

Prepare, bake, and cool one 9-inch pie shell (a butter-based crust tastes best with lemon pie).

Filling:
1 cup sugar
4½ tablespoons cornstarch
Grated rind plus juice of 1 large lemon
3 egg yolks (reserve whites for meringue)
2 cups boiling water
1 tablespoon butter
Meringue:
⅓ cup sugar
1 teaspoon cornstarch
¼ teaspoon cream of tartar
3 egg whites

In a heavy saucepan, stir together 1 cup sugar and 4½ tablespoons cornstarch. Add lemon rind and juice and beaten egg yolks; stir together well. While stirring briskly, gradually add boiling water. Continue to stir gently as you bring mixture to full boil over medium heat. Remove from heat and stir in butter. Pour into prepared pie shell.

Preheat oven to 300 degrees F. Combine ⅓ cup sugar, 1 teaspoon cornstarch, and cream of tartar. Beat egg whites until stiff; add sugar mixture gradually and beat until incorporated. Dollop meringue over filled pie, then spread to cover filling, making sure to seal to edges of pie crust. Bake in preheated oven for 15 minutes. Turn off heat, open oven door, and let pie cool gradually for 10 minutes. Remove to cooling rack and cool completely before serving.

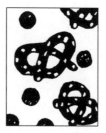

Muse-Food for Writers

By Chris Crowe

Most writers have mastered the difficult art of *not* writing. People who aren't writers think that *not* writing is simply a matter of laziness or procrastination, but obviously they don't appreciate the subtle complexities of *not* writing. Real writers know that *not* writing requires much more energy and creativity than writing does. In order to *not* write, authors must find other activities to take the place of writing, important tasks like rearranging their desks, preparing Sunday School lessons, paying bills, balancing the checkbook, searching for lost socks, shooting baskets with the kids, talking on the phone, and writing letters (a particularly good activity because it *looks* as if you're writing).

As a Mormon, I have lots of experience in procrastination (especially where home teaching is concerned). As a Mormon writer, I have extensive experience in *not* writing, having mastered it during high school when I spent much of my time doing anything except writing required assignments. Back then, it was easy to avoid working on essays or reports simply by hanging out with friends, watching TV, working out, cruising, or any one of hundreds of things high school kids still do to kill time. These avoidance tactics also served me well in college, but as time passed and my interests changed, I decided, ironically enough, that I wanted to be a writer.

I soon found that most published writers are also masters of *not* writing, but they're *published* writers because somehow they manage to do the dirty work of writing even when they don't feel like it. The logic was inescapable: in order to be a writer, I too would have to write. I immediately started looking for ways to overcome *not* writing.

I read books about writing, tried exercises, positive mental attitudes, goal setting, Franklin planning, soothing background music, free writing, ergonomic chairs, handwriting, typewriting, word processing. Unfortunately, none of these had any lasting effect, and I worried that I was doomed to a career of *not* writing. Seeing my hopes dashed like an overripe Halloween pumpkin, I became depressed. And, being depressed, I turned to what I always turn to when I'm in the depths of despair:

Food. Food became my writing muse!

I discovered muse-food several years ago while struggling to get a book written. Writing a book is tedious, depressing, and unpleasant. It's like not only having to eat liver and onions every day but also having to prepare them. Faced with the unpleasant task of writing a book, my avoidance behaviors of *not* writing proliferated like mold on a week-old uncovered casserole: my desk was immaculate, my checkbook was balanced, and every sock in the house lived snugly with its mate. Knowing that my career as a writer depended on my actually writing, I desperately searched for motivational tricks to keep my nose to the keyboard. Nothing worked until, depressed with failure, I tried rewarding myself for getting little bits of writing done.

We had recently potty trained our son by giving him an M&M each time he sat on the toilet and took care of business. The reward system worked for him, so I bought a package of gourmet chocolate-covered almonds (writing, after all, is more sophisticated than pottying) and allowed myself to eat one each time I completed a page of the book.

It worked. My almond-per-page diet got me through the book. I tried it with other writing projects and found that it worked on those as well. Muse-food cured me.

Not all foods qualify as muse-food. I quickly discovered that soups and salads, though healthy and tasty, were more distraction than inspiration. Besides that, soup, bacon bits, vegetable debris, and salad dressing really aren't good for computer keyboards. Pastas also failed the muse-food test. Rice, breakfast cereal, fruits that had to be peeled, tacos, pita pockets, pizza, scrambled eggs, and many other foods also proved to be more trouble than they were worth. Gooey, sticky, or slimy foods, or any food that required a fork, spoon, knife, chopstick, plate, or bowl, just didn't cut it at the keyboard.

The best muse-foods are tasty, bite-sized morsels that don't droop or drip and can be eaten one-handed. My favorites are still gourmet chocolate-covered almonds, but it's difficult to justify such an extravagance to my wife and kids, who, when they see me at the computer for hours popping chocolate-covered almonds, are convinced that I'm not really working. M&Ms are a good substitute. Other good muse-foods include Pringles, pretzels, caramel corn, Chex snack mix, peanuts (plain, dry-roasted, honey-roasted, or toffee-covered), popcorn, Wheat Thins, cookies, malted milk balls, jelly beans, and other bite-sized unwrapped candies.

There are, unfortunately, some down sides to muse-foods. One is weight gain. A writer addicted to muse-food may soon look like a trucker hooked on Jolt Cola and Big Macs. When I'm fighting both my weight and a writing deadline, I like grapes, raisins, dates, baby carrots, dried pineapple chunks, pickles, olives, and apples.

But the real problem with muse-food is that for writers predisposed to *not* writing, muse-food can turn from cure to cause. For me, searching for and preparing muse-food gradually became an elaborate avoidance tactic. Nowadays, I rarely work at home because the Siren's call of the kitchen makes it impossible for me to get any writing done. At home, I would wander into the kitchen looking for muse-food to get me going, but, once there, I'd find plenty of things to keep me from writing. Instead of store-bought cookies, why not whip up a batch of homemade ones? Instead of eating plain peanuts, why not make chocolate-covered peanuts myself? And why eat grapes when I can get out the fruit dryer and make my own raisins?

As a writer, I have now come full circle. You may think that I've overcome *not* writing, and I have, but as a Mormon, I have been conditioned that nearly everything is an excuse for eating, and that, unfortunately, is what writing has become for me. I'm afraid that in the long run, my reliance on muse-food will have a heavy impact on me as a writer, and that if I ever tackle a major work, neither my heart, my belt, nor my writing chair will bear it. William Faulkner, not being Mormon, insisted that in addition to needing food to write, he needed "tobacco and a little whiskey." Imagine what he might have written had he discovered gourmet chocolate-covered almonds.

Note: This essay was inspired and fueled by a pair of Grandma's Home-Style Fudge Chocolate-Chip Cookies and by half a box of Crunch 'n' Munch Buttery Toffee Popcorn with Peanuts.

MUSE-FOOD POTPOURRI FOR WRITERS

In a large bowl, gently combine the following:

1 can Pringles (any style)
1 container (any size) malted milk balls
1 package (16 ounces) M&Ms
2 cups mini-pretzels
3 cups dry-roasted peanuts

Help yourself to one handful every completed page or every 5 minutes (whichever is sooner). This recipe may also be used for readers.

Sunday Dinner

By Claudia Bushman

I love to remember the Sunday dinners of my childhood. We dined from our best dishes set on linen cloths in our formal dining room. My mother, Jean Gordon Lauper, a formidable hostess, would make many arrangements in advance and later zip home from church, after leading the congregational music and usually the choir numbers as well, to preside graciously over a beautiful and tasty repast.

Our dinner table in San Francisco, far removed from Salt Lake City, centered on Church activities. My father was always the bishop, a member of the stake presidency, or the patriarch, and we often entertained visiting Church officials in the intervals between conference meetings. In those days the First Presidency and the Twelve traveled more frequently to fewer stakes, and every Church President from Heber J. Grant on, as well as many other leaders, turned up at our table. I doubt that many members of the Church saw as many officials as we did in those days.

My three sisters and I listened to those seasoned and entertaining leaders tell informal stories we never heard from the stand. Sometimes they engaged us directly, and I cherish some exchanges I had with the wise and good Elder George Albert Smith when he was still an apostle. I prayed that he would be the next President of the Church, and, ignorant of the traditions of seniority, I felt that my prayers were answered when he was later sustained.

My mother prepared simple and delicious food—not too contrived, not too expensive, not too many dishes. We never had chicken, which looked too much like a real animal to her. A ham was anonymous enough, as was a large pot roast, and she was known to serve stews, meat loaves, and even large tureens of split pea soup. One of those succulent main dishes, accompanied by potatoes, vegetables, a green salad, and her legendary baking-powder biscuits, would make up the main course.

Her desserts were something else, extravagant and elaborate. She made delicious layer cakes from scratch, often decorating them in enchanting ways. Beneath her skillful hands, a cake's white icing would be covered with green-tinted coconut with nests of eggs hidden in the grass and ducks swimming on mirror-ponds. She turned out rich cookies almost as fast as we could eat them and would frequently whip up a pan of brownies or a platter of fudge or fondant as an extra. Another treat was a delicious crumb cake. Surprisingly moist and simple, this cake is still a family favorite. Strawberry pie was another of mother's triumphs.

We had wonderful Sunday dinners even when no General Authorities were in sight. My mother would frequently tell us on Sunday mornings, "Now, girls, we have a particularly good dinner today. You may each invite one guest." These invitations, given out at church to males only, were keenly sought. We would invite current boyfriends, pals, and good company, and we certainly sought out interesting strangers should any be present. At these dinners, our conversation was unrestrained, and we leapt from topic to topic with lightning speed. Some guests found this verbal banter cruel and intimidating, but it was certainly fun for us.

After dinner, the girls and the guests would clean up the kitchen, sending the parents off to nap and read the paper. Then we set off on an outing. Sometimes we would go to one of San Francisco's museums, concentrating on the armor, the ship models, the Impressionists, or some special exhibition. We often went to Golden Gate Park to stroll through the Arboretum, the Shakespeare Garden, or the Japanese Tea Garden. Another favorite destination was Sigmund Stern Grove, an estate where free concerts were presented each Sunday afternoon. Our happy group would sit on the grass, if we could not get chairs, listening to visiting orchestras and chamber groups and sometimes watching the ballet. We felt ourselves culturally superior. After this, in those days, we went back to sacrament meeting in the evening.

I loved those Sunday dinners and have felt that my own were lacking in comparison. I did decide that time, energy, and money could be saved by serving a fancy brunch instead of a Sunday dinner, and I managed that for some years. The children and I kept up some cultural Sunday activities, frequently visiting the Boston Museum of Fine Arts, surveying the glass flowers, or walking the Freedom Trail, sometimes under duress.

We seldom spent our Sundays doing genealogy, writing to the missionaries, or reading the scriptures, and we didn't even visit the sick, widows, and fatherless very often. But our Sundays were wonderfully high-minded and enjoyable. How true that happy memories are flavored with the foods of childhood.

Ann Barton's Crumb Cake

Mix:
⅞ cup oil
1 cup brown sugar
½ cup white sugar
2 cups flour
1 teaspoon salt

Reserve about 3 tablespoons of the mixture for topping. Add to the remainder:

1 teaspoon baking soda
1 teaspoon nutmeg
1 egg
1 cup sour milk (may use 1 cup milk soured with 1 tablespoon vinegar)

Mix well and pour into a 9 x 13-inch pan.
To the reserved crumbs, add a handful of broken walnuts and 1 teaspoon cinnamon. Sprinkle the crumbs on top of the batter and bake at 325 degrees F. for 45 minutes.

Jean Gordon Lauper's Strawberry Pie

One baked pie shell (The secret to my mother's excellent pie crust was to work the butter into the flour with a pastry blender in two phases: the first half until fine like cornmeal—for tenderness—and the second half until the size of small peas—for flakiness.)

Enough beautiful whole strawberries to be arranged in two layers in the shell.

Simmer 2 cups less attractive berries in 2 cups water until soft and faded. Fish out and discard berries. Add 1 cup sugar mixed with 3 tablespoons cornstarch to the juice, cooking and stirring until the mixture is thick and clear. Add coloring and vanilla or lemon flavoring if desired.

Cool the sauce, spoon over the berries in the pie shell, and refrigerate.

Swedish fruit-flavored cornstarch puddings could be used for the same effect.

This wondrous dessert, topped generously with whipped cream, gave the impression of wholesomeness while being luscious in the extreme.

My Mother's Memory

By Louise Plummer

Last week when my parents came to dinner, my mother handed me a pink sheet of paper. It was her ward's Relief Society newsletter. Her name appeared under "Sister Spotlight" in bold type. "Have I given you a copy of this?" Mother asked, her face eager. She pointed at her name under the Sister Spotlight and read, "She was born in Breukelen, Utrecht, The Netherlands."

I shook my head. "No, you haven't," I said. I read through the short biography. "This is great!" I said, tacking it onto the bulletin board in my kitchen. She looked pleased.

This was the third time she had given me this same

newsletter. My mother is seventy-five years old, and she is losing her memory. I am the last in my large family to admit this. Only now have I dared to write it: my mother is losing her memory. At first it irritated my father. "I have to repeat things a dozen times. She asks me what show is on television, and I tell her, and five minutes later she asks me again." But this and other examples like it didn't seem sufficient evidence. She probably wasn't listening the first time, I thought. I do that myself. "Why don't you take her to Al?" I suggested. "He can tell you if it's serious." Al is a neurologist friend of ours.

My father took Mother to see Al. He said that Mother, at worst, was marginal, but suggested that she be tested by a psychologist. He named someone who, as it happened, wasn't covered on my parents' insurance. "It costs $250," my father told me over the phone.

"You can afford that, can't you?"

"I guess," was all he said, but he never made an appointment.

Later, my father and mother took some visiting Dutch relatives down to St. George and checked into a motel with a kitchenette. After they had unpacked, they went out for groceries. On the way back to the motel, my mother, looking anxious, turned to my father and said, "Shouldn't we check into a motel before it gets too late?"

"We checked into a motel an hour ago; don't you remember?"

She looked confused. "We did?"

"You unpacked the clothes."

"I don't remember," she said.

Not long ago, she told my father that she couldn't remember their wedding day.

"You don't think we've just been living together for fifty-five years, do you?" my father asked.

She smirked at him, probably. I wasn't there. "I know we're married," she said. "I just can't remember getting married."

Even now as I write these examples of her memory loss, I want to deny them. I want to break in with opposing evidence: she still manages the family finances, writes all the checks, and keeps the budget without making mistakes. She still works in the temple, remembering the complicated lines of her assignments. Doesn't this prove there's nothing seriously wrong?

Last summer our entire extended family was at Bear Lake. On my night to cook, I made sloppy joes. Actually, I didn't "make" anything. I fried hamburger and opened a half dozen cans of Hunt's Sloppy Joe Sauce and poured them onto the cooked hamburger. Then I spooned the mixture onto hamburger buns. Not a very big culinary deal.

My mother thought the sloppy joes were delicious.

"Really?" I asked her.

"I love these," she said, taking another bite.

"Well," I said. "I was a little embarrassed to make them, because your recipe is the best I've ever tasted."

"My recipe?" Her eyes seemed to search the past.

"Best sloppy joes in the world," I said. "You would simmer it all afternoon and then we'd put the whole pot in the car and go to George Washington Park and have a picnic. You always made a red Jello salad with whipping cream mixed into it. That's still my favorite way to have Jello."

Her nod was hesitant. "I didn't know I made sloppy joes." She shrugged her shoulders and giggled. I giggled with her. What else was there to do?

Then she forgot the Appelflappen. All my growing-up years, my mother spent New Year's Eve Day making Appelflappen. They are cored apple slices dipped in pancake batter and deep-fried like doughnuts to a golden brown. That's the extent of the recipe. We kids fought over who got to sift the powdered sugar over them. To make and eat Appelflappen during New Year's is as Dutch as wooden shoes.

Last Christmas my mother volunteered to bring Appelflappen to a holiday party with Dutch friends. On the afternoon of the party, my father asked, "Aren't you supposed to bring Appelflappen to the party?"

"Oh, I forgot," Mother said, and went about making up the pancake batter. My father had an unfinished project out in the garage, which he went to complete. When he returned, Mother had made, not Appelflappen, but a huge stack of pancakes.

When my father told me this story, he told not only of her confusion but of her mortification at making such a foolish mistake. She has memory enough to be embarrassed.

Now I talk to her in stories. "Remember when Marva Johnson slept over on New Year's Eve and you made Appelflappen—and Gerard took our picture with my Brownie camera and—" I continue, relishing the details, using my most animated voice, until the story is finished.

Often she laughs as if she's hearing it for the first time.

RETIRED FROM BREAKFAST

BY DELYS WAITE COWLES

At one time distant in my memory, when my children weren't in school and my husband was, I dutifully arose every morning to fix a full breakfast. This was when we were in our twenties and thin and no one had to be anywhere until 9:00 A.M.

I was just copying what I had seen my whole life. My mother cooked healthy food. She made oatmeal or Cream of Wheat, and we were allowed a little bit of sugar for flavoring. On rushed days she would make us a breakfast eggnog that we would gulp down on our way out to early-morning seminary. Sometimes she would indulge us with pancakes or French toast, but whatever she made, it was hot and good and nourishing.

The one luxury she never bought was cold cereal. Other kids stocked up on Cap'n Crunch and Lucky Charms every morning, but not us. Sweetened cereal was not allowed. Neither was white bread or the phrase "shut up." The only time we got sugared cereal was when we went camping. Mom would buy the variety pack, and we would all grab the Frosted Flakes and the Fruit Loops first, and the loser got the Special K. Then we would open the small, wax-paper-lined boxes and pour the milk right in. Ah, decadence.

When my daughters started school, I wanted to continue to make great breakfasts just like Mom. But then I had another baby and had to nurse him first thing in the morning. And it took time to bundle my daughters in sweaters, coats, scarves, leg warmers, boots, hats, and mittens before the bus came. My time for breakfast preparation shrank to be so small that I did the unthinkable: I bought cold cereal. But I did have my standards. I bought the ones with no sugar added— Cheerios and Rice Krispies.

These days, with two more children and other professional demands, I am lucky to find time to pour a bowlful and feed myself, let alone six other people. So breakfast is a free-for-all. You want it, you make it.

With me as Mom, our breakfast repertoire consists of generic-brand toasted oats and crispy rice bought in bulk and poured into plastic containers, varied with microwave oatmeal or Cream of Wheat. There is one more dish we have, and this takes care of all the guilt I have over not making breakfast. It's homemade granola. I make it only once every five months or so, but when this granola is around, none of the kids ask what they can have. They just go for a bowl of granola, with or without milk.

Oh, yes, when we visit Grandma she still cooks fantastic breakfasts, all of the food low-fat and healthy. But now she pulls me aside and confesses, "Delys, when all the children and grandchildren aren't here, Dad and I eat mostly oatmeal these days. Cooked in the microwave."

BREAKFAST GRANOLA

(For my big family I double or quadruple the recipe)

Mix together:
6 cups quick cooking oats
1 cup wheat germ
½ cup sesame seeds
½ cup raw sunflower seeds
1 cup chopped walnuts
1 cup chopped almonds or cashews
½ teaspoon salt
In a saucepan, combine:
1 cup water
½ cup vegetable oil
1 cup brown sugar
¼ cup honey
¼ cup molasses
1 teaspoon cinnamon

Stir over medium heat until sugar is dissolved. Pour the syrup over the dry mixture and stir until all is moistened. Spread on one or two cookie sheets and bake at 275 degrees F. for about an hour, stirring once. Store in a plastic container. Serve with raisins and milk.

Warning: If you let your children snack on the granola after school, the cereal will last only a few days, so be prepared to make more next time.

RECIPE FOR 2:00 A.M. DRIVING

BY STEVE WALKER

We've all been there: the 2:00 A.M. struggle to keep awake driving through the never-ending nighttime expanses of someplace like the monotonous middle of the Mojave Desert with no company but that repetitive yellow line, vision blurry, lids droopy, back achy, neck smooshy, head heavy. What's a Mormon to do?

It's serious business, actually. "Dozing and driving is every bit as dangerous as drinking and driving," according to BYU Wellness Program's *You Snooze, You Lose* brochure. "Sleepy drivers probably cause 57 percent of all fatal accidents." Sleepy driving may be even more serious a matter for Mormons than for other drivers:

"At BYU, dozing and driving is the number-one cause of death."

I confess. In the past I succumbed to the occasional Diet Dr. Pepper.

And, oh wow, did it work. Two sips and I was back, bright-eyed and eager, the highway no longer an unbearable burden but a yellow brick road stretching toward the happy possibilities of Disneyland. Once I even ventured as far as a Jolt Cola—"twice the caffeine"—and felt no need of sleep at all for several days.

Since those days, however, I have decided to eschew the most common waker-upper, caffeine. If I am disadvantaged by this moratorium, then I comfort myself knowing that God has provided alternatives.

You're familiar with some of them. Sticking your head out the window like a dog. Slapping yourself in imitation of Curly of the Three Stooges. Singing at the top of your voice old show tunes: "Some Enchanted Evening," maybe, or "Oklahoma," or my personal favorite, "Old Man River." Such approaches are at best clumsy and at worst unreliable. I once drifted off right in the middle of an Elvis Presleyish rendition of "You get a little drunk / And you land in jai-ail" while hanging my head out the window and slapping my cheeks.

There's a better substitute: food. My careful scientific observation over half a century of tired driving has pinpointed the wake-up effectiveness rating of anything you can put in your mouth. Liquids, for instance, have the advantage of ready availability—readier than caffeine. They replace lost electrolytes and make you cheerier. What is more, liquids put increasing pressure on the bladder, which can provide a stimulus to stop, get out, and otherwise wake up.

But stopping to go every fifteen miles can get irritating. Something chewable is better. The cracklier-crunchier here, the more texturally interesting, the more effective. Celery works well, as does caramel popcorn. Classiest is Jordan almonds. But there is in chewables, too, a disadvantage, a kind of law of diminishing returns: You get too full, you get sleepy. Experts talk of turkey tryptophan as the source of Thanksgiving sleepiness; I'm pretty sure the actual problem is volume.

There's a principle in that: Spread it out. On the road eat a little over a long time, simulating as closely as you can the intravenous drip.

That makes the ultimate form of waker-upper sugar. You can get it in many forms—fruits work well, or vegetables. I suspect the waker-upper many people get in that late-night cup of coffee may be as much the sugar as the caffeine. But sugar is most effective in its purest form: Twizzlers strawberry licorice. Driving straight through from Provo to Boston—and with far fewer of those headachy, shaky side effects—a stick of Twizzlers red licorice every twelve minutes.

That's my recipe for antidrowsiness on the road, a recipe backed by experimentation of such extent and care as to make it closer to a prescription. This is the precise formula for a body weight of 150 pounds. If you're bigger, you get to eat more.

One stick
Twizzlers strawberry licorice
Every twelve minutes

This is hard-won wisdom, earned mile by mile on many a bad road on many a dark night. Twizzlers will keep you awake. Maybe it's the sugar. Probably it's the red dye. Whatever it is, it works.

SETTIN' PRETTY: JAN'S RED JELLO

BY ANN GARDNER STONE

I know what you're thinking. It's the obligatory Jello essay—the one that makes fun of that bouncy, gelatinous concoction. Jello has become a quasi-religious symbol that crosses all denominational boundaries to find its way onto every potluck supper table in congregations across the country. It's an easy target for jokes and ridicule. However, this isn't *that* kind of Jello essay or Jello recipe. I am here to speak in behalf of Jello—more particularly, Jan's Red Jello. This is more than the quivering square of salad on the left side of the dinner plate. Jan's Red Jello is friends, family, and tradition.

We have lived in the Midwest for more than twenty-five years. During that time we have spent fewer than five holiday dinners with immediate family in Arizona. When we moved to Chicago, one of the first couples we met were the Fritzes—Jan and Dale. We started sharing a holiday table with the Fritzes when the hassle of holiday travel with small children became overwhelming and expensive. It started as occasional and unofficial—a substitute for faraway family—and has become traditional and established, more familiar to our children than a celebration with grandparents.

Sometime during the twenty-five years, Jan and Dale moved to Milwaukee, but that is only ninety miles of toll road away and has not interfered with our holiday schedule. We have developed a system of alternating hosting duties for Thanksgiving and Christmas, although we are not slaves to this schedule and we rearrange and adjust as circumstances demand.

There was one Christmas when Jan got the flu on Christmas Eve, and because it was her turn to prepare most of the meal, we had to find our Christmas dinner elsewhere. The only restaurant we found open on Christmas Day was a Jewish deli, so Christmas dinner was matzo ball soup and pastrami sandwiches.

We still laugh about the year I miscalculated minutes per pound of cooking time for the Thanksgiving turkey. Math not being my strong suit, I popped the bird in the oven at noon expecting it to be done by 2:30. We ate a rather sad and lonely turkey at about 6:00 P.M., having devoured the rest of the meal well before that poor bird made its appearance.

One year, Jan (or Dale—this has never been clearly

established) left the bag with the rolls and dessert by the back door and drove the ninety miles to Chicago before discovering the omission. We found Twinkies and some day-old packaged rolls at the local convenience store, and our kids were particularly charmed by the idea of Christmas Twinkies.

The year my husband died, 1983, was one of Chicago's coldest. Car batteries were rebelling, especially the one in our courageous '69 Impala. In the true spirit of stewardship, my home teacher came over on Christmas Eve, removed the battery from my car, and kept it charging in his basement overnight. He replaced it on Christmas morning so that my sons and I could make the trip to Milwaukee for our traditional Christmas dinner. It seemed particularly important to be together with the Fritzes that year.

Menus have remained somewhat traditional—turkey on Thanksgiving, ham or tenderloin or sometimes a pork roast for Christmas. The side dishes change with the latest new recipe or cooking class at Relief Society. But the one constant has always been Jan's Red Jello. Perhaps it is the festive color or the ease of preparation that makes it a staple. The strawberries certainly add flair, and that layer of sour cream is definitely a plus. Whatever the reason, the red Jello is always part of our shared meal. Even the busy year that Jan had the entire Thanksgiving dinner catered, we had red Jello. Jan always prepares it, and we don't even mention it anymore as we plan the menu for the upcoming occasion. Red Jello is just a given.

And after twenty-five years, Jan and Dale and their children have become a "given" for me and my sons. We are no longer just substitutes for faraway families— we are family. I love and miss my Arizona family and make as many trips to see them as time and budget will allow. But I have learned that *family* need not be so narrowly defined, that joy, love, and shared traditions can be developed and nurtured within a wider circle. I know how the student couples feel who drop into our community for a brief time and yearn their whole stay for families back West. I too yearned those first few years and plotted and planned ways that we could move back "home." It took me a while to realize that all that time we were building "home" here.

Our holiday dinners have remained the central get-togethers with the Fritzes, but no longer the only ones. We have shared baptisms, graduations, illnesses, missionary farewells, and one long week between my husband's death and his funeral when Jan drove back and forth between Milwaukee and Chicago every day to make me laugh when I thought it was no longer possible. Although most of that week is an unpleasant blur, I do have some vivid memories: love and support unselfishly given, kind words spoken, memories of Dan shared. And I remember the funeral meal. The table was piled high with rolls and ham and scalloped potatoes and wonderful desserts, but what caught my eye were shimmering ruby squares, red as valentine hearts—Jan's Red Jello.

JAN'S RED JELLO

1 package (3 ounces) strawberry Jello
2 cups boiling water
2 packages (10 ounces each) frozen strawberries
1 can (10½ ounces) crushed pineapple with juice
1 cup sour cream

Dissolve strawberry Jello in the boiling water. Add the frozen strawberries. Stir until strawberries are thawed. Add the pineapple and juice and mix well. Pour half the mixture into an 8-inch square pan and chill until firm. Spread sour cream evenly over the set Jello. Pour the rest of the Jello mixture on top and chill until firm. Cut into 9 squares. Top each with a dollop of sour cream and a fresh strawberry, if available.

Icebox Cake

By Elouise Bell

To say that my father wasn't much of a cook is like saying that I am not much of a trapeze artist. You could pile up negatives a long time and still not come close to the full inadequacy in either case. Yet it was my father who taught me to make one of the few dishes for which I get more from dinner guests than a no-teeth smile and a change of subject. Icebox Cake is as simple as food preparation gets—and it involves NO cooking.

Truth is, Dad cooked about as often as I swung from a trapeze. When I was a child, fathers didn't cook. I have exactly one memory of such an oddity. Mother was in a hospital in Philadelphia. Dad decided to make gravy to go with the hamburgers and mashed potatoes he had made for supper. Mom's recipe for gravy clearly said, "Two tablespoons of flour."

110

"Nonsense!" snorted Dad. He was making supper for a teenaged boy given to muscle building, a preteen boy on the short and scrawny side, determined to eat his way to manhood, and a seven-year-old who had yet to meet a carbohydrate she didn't like. Two tablespoons indeed! He measured out two heaping *cups* of flour and stirred it into the hot milk in the frying pan. As soon as it bubbled, he turned it off and set it before us in a Pyrex bowl.

"Blech!" said one of the children (nameless here and forevermore). "It tastes like library paste!"

"Hush up and eat!" came the answer. And then *he* tasted it. One look warned us not to say a word, then or when Mother returned.

Dad knew nothing about gravy, except that he liked it. But he did know how to put together something that was called, in those days, Icebox Cake. It was, and is, as easy to make as a peanut butter and jelly sandwich, and far more delicious.

But before I give you the instructions, permit a digression, a ramble down Nostalgia Lane. How many of you remember iceboxes? Raise your hands. Well, in the days before refrigerators, which is to say before 1950, people kept food more or less cool in cabinets designed to hold blocks of ice: hence the term "icebox." I have yet to meet anyone who remembers those days who doesn't smile happily when recalling the romance, no, not of the icebox itself, which was a nuisance, but of the Iceman.

The homely ritual of filling the icebox began with

the *sign,* a piece of cardboard about a foot square, marked off into four triangles, one base on each side of the square. Each triangle was a different color and had a different number in the middle in large print: 25, 50, 75, 100. If your mother wanted, say, 50 pounds of ice, she would turn the side so that the 50 triangle was at the top. She placed the sign in a window facing the street. On the appointed day, the huge ice truck would rattle into your street. (I think I even remember horse-drawn trucks, but I won't swear to that. My friend Elizabeth, a few years younger than I, definitely remembers the horses: she pestered until she was allowed to ride with the driver.) The Iceman would glance at the sign in each window and deliver the required amounts up and down the block. Finally you would hear him lumbering up your stairs. BANG! No polite knock this. You scurried to open the door, and there he was.

Most often the Iceman was a burly fellow who in the course of a day carried tons of ice to houses and apartments on the routes. He did not dress like a salesman, or like the dry-cleaning man or the baker or the milkman who came to the door. He wore rough pants and most often a T-shirt, stained and sweat-soaked. A small square of leather perched on the Iceman's shoulder for the block of ice to rest on. Another rectangle of leather draped from his waist, but no kin to your mother's aprons. With his great boots and his mighty gloves, he always seemed bigger and somehow more real than anyone or anything else in your house. With one hand he unlatched the icebox door (unless you had leaped to do it first), and then, with the huge pincers of his ice tongs, he swung the dripping block of ice neatly into its compartment in the cabinet, pushed the door shut with the meaty heel of his hand, touched his cap to your mother, and was gone.

But the best part of the ritual was yet to come. You scampered down after him to his big ice wagon, and before driving out of your street, he would toss small broken bits of ice to you and the other waiting kids. If he was truly an Iceman of character, who took his responsibilities as Hero seriously, he would whip out his long deadly ice pick from its sheath—it was three times the size of your father's kitchen ice pick—and ka-chink! ka-chink! ka-chunk! he'd hack some pieces from a solid block of ice and throw you a big one. Most kids brought an old frayed washcloth to the wagon. You put your bit of ice in the cloth and walked away happily, slowly sucking the ice and watching the truck trail ice water and flecks of sawdust as it rumbled away until next week.

The rest of the week, you lived with the nuisance part of the icebox: the *pan.*

"Have you checked the pan?" your mother would ask at least once a day. You'd better have, because if it was your chore and you *forgot* to check the pan that rested on the floor beneath the icebox drain to catch the melting water, there would be a flood. With your luck, the pan would overflow at the very moment your mother's friends were coming into the kitchen to sample her coffee cake. Or, if you were really unlucky, disaster would spread as your father paddled into the kitchen in his stocking feet on Sunday morning.

So you checked the pan a lot, and when it was nearly full, you slid it out and carried it to the sink to empty it—quickly, because the water from the icebox was now draining onto the floor, but slowly, because if you ran, the contents would start sloshing and then spilling. Swinging on a trapeze may take some doing, but for learning balance, coordination, and timing, I say emptying the icebox pan had no equal.

How to Make Icebox Cake

Icebox Cake, which my father loved and encouraged me to make from time to time, has no recipe as such, but instructions follow. An eight-year-old can make a fine Icebox Cake. To begin, you need a box of Nabisco Famous Chocolate Wafers. Other cookies won't work, so don't try them. The cookies come in a box with a cellophane window so you can see them clearly. The wafers are dark chocolate and very thin. They have no doodads on or in them— no chocolate chips, nuts, raisins, frosting, coconut— zip. Just be careful; don't break too many of the fragile wafers before building the cake. Breaking one or two, of course, is the chef's prerogative: there is nothing to do with the broken wafers but eat them and get them out of your way.

Next, whip up a pint of heavy cream. In case there are any eight-year-olds reading this, note that cream whips best if the bowl and the beaters are chilled and perfectly free of any speck of oil before you start. Now, the recipe on the cookie box does not call for sugar to be added to the cream as you whip it, only vanilla. But add a tablespoon or so of sugar anyway. Now you have a box of wafers and a bowl of stiffly whipped cream. Take a wafer, slather cream on it, put another wafer on top, slather cream on that, and continue. When you have a stack of half a dozen cream-covered wafers, set the stack on a plate and continue to build a new stack. When finished, assemble all the stacks into one long log on your serving plate. Now slather more cream on the outside of the log. Swirl the cream nicely, being sure to cover all the brown spots of cookie showing through. Put the assembled log into the fridge (formerly the icebox) for about six hours. During this time, the crisp cookies soak up the cream and turn into cake.

When you are ready to serve, decorate the top of the cake with chocolate sprinkles or whatever you like. I just recently discovered Betty Crocker's All-Chocolate Decorations. These are little pieces of chocolate in the shape of pretty leaves; they look enticing on the top of the log. Slice the cake at an angle—that part is important—and fairly thin, because it is so rich. The result will be a zebra-striped slice of cake that is delicious. One box of wafers serves about a dozen guests or six family members.

CULINARY
COMPATIBILITY

BY KATHRYN H. KIDD

Because I didn't get married until the ancient age of twenty-six, I had plenty of time to decide what I wanted in a husband. When I was young, I wanted him tall, dark, handsome, and rich. When I got a little older, I set new standards—he had to be a good church member, have a sense of humor, have an I.Q. greater than that of your average mailbox, and hate football. Now that I have the perspective of experience and age, I realize there was one important qualification that should have been on my list but wasn't. I'm talking about culinary compatibility.

I always knew that marriage involves compromise, as two people with diverse backgrounds come together to start their own traditions. But I thought of these adjustments more in terms of deciding where to squeeze the toothpaste tube or choosing which person got which side of the bed. I didn't realize one of the largest areas of adjustment would be in the culture of mealtime and food.

I've been told I'm a terrific cook, and, in fact, my fried chicken is legendary. I had years of practice in the art of cooking balanced meals. But once I was living alone, I learned to eat the way my body wanted me to eat. I would stop on the way home from work and haunt the local supermarket, stalking up and down the aisles like a hungry lion after prey. Eventually something always caught my eye. One night it might be spinach. The next night it could be oysters. Maybe the next night it would be spinach again. If I was in the mood for something, that was all I wanted to eat. I enjoyed the taste of food, but food was only sustenance. I cooked it and ate it and cleaned up after it; then I went on with my life.

The first night I cooked dinner for Clark, I created some sort of one-dish meal. I served him a big plate of whatever it was, and he looked balefully up at me.

"Where's the rest of it?"

He went on to explain that a proper meal consisted of a main course, a vegetable, some sort of bread or starch, and a dessert. I admitted that the concept of dessert was new to me, but I pointed out that my one-dish meal contained meat, pasta, and vegetables. "That doesn't count," he said patiently. "If it's all mixed together, it's one item. Dinner has four items."

As the days progressed, I learned there were other rules. He doesn't eat food that looks like a recognizable part of an animal. (So much for my famous fried chicken!) He doesn't eat dark meat even if it has been cut off the chicken or turkey "because it has yucky things in it." The very first time I ever cooked seafood for him, he looked up at me with round eyes and said, in a voice of utter hopelessness, "Fish *again?*"

Before the advent of Mad Cow Disease, beef used to be acceptable, but only in quantities that could best be described as "microscopic." Once I ordered steaks from the Omaha Steak Company, which are the smallest pieces of meat that could possibly be described as coming in a steak shape. Clark took one look at the priceless morsels and asked, "Can't we cut 'em up for stir-fry?"

There are foods he officially doesn't like and won't eat, even though he's never tasted them. He once ate a whole bowl of crawfish tails, thinking they were shrimp. When he complimented me on the great shrimp and learned he'd been eating crawfish, he refused to eat another bite. Every time I have asked if he wanted okra for dinner, he has pleaded with me not to cook it. But when I cook it without asking him first, he eats more of it than I do. His mouth and his eyes are not synchronized, and this is a trial for him.

He loves vegetables, especially if they're in the shape of potatoes or corn. He could eat corn on the cob every night during the summer. Corn just isn't high on my agenda. It makes more of a mess than it's worth. But he asks for so little that we have corn several times a week during the summer. We customarily eat salad with the corn, even though salad always makes me sick.

For me the hardest part of learning to cook for two was accepting that dessert is the base of Clark's food pyramid. I've never understood why a person would want something else after dinner is over and he's no longer hungry. Clark has some scientific theory about how dinner makes lumps in your stomach, and ice cream slides down between the cracks. He's the one with the science degree; I just have to accept that he knows what he's talking about. I only wish he'd find a theory to explain his attraction to sweet rolls.

Clark's theory is that there's always room for sugar. He made a casserole for our dinner once. There was some sort of meat in it, and mushrooms, and several kinds of vegetables, and probably some sort of cream-based soup. He'd seasoned it with salt and lots of garlic—and then he added a liberal dose of chocolate chips. It made for an interesting dinner.

We weren't married long before we realized that a compromise of some sort had to be made. We both signed up for cooking classes through community education. Clark became a fine Oriental cook, while I eventually specialized in Mexican cuisine. After our cooking classes we had several years of enjoyable meals. Then we moved to Virginia, where Church callings take so much of our time that we don't have the extra hours to spend in the kitchen.

In the course of more than twenty years of marriage,

we've developed a Kidd family law regarding food. In our family, the person who likes something the most gets to eat it. I get the bigger slice of meat; he gets most of the dessert. He lets me have *all* the pickled okra and anything that looks like an oyster, which is downright civilized of him. Any pastries brought into the house are consumed by Clark, which is no less civilized of me.

We've been married long enough to find recipes we both enjoy, but the best solution we've ever discovered takes American Express. The older we get, the more we eat out. We find places where Clark can get his salads and breads, and where I can have oysters or boiled cabbage as the spirit prompts me. Most of our friends eat in restaurants once or twice a year. Clark and I eat out several times a week. Our friends think we're indulging ourselves. Actually, we're surviving the only way we know how.

Truth be told, culinary compatibility is probably an international problem. At this very moment, somewhere a man is looking with hopeless eyes at the new wife who has just put couscous before him for the very first time. I can just hear him saying balefully, "Couscous *again?*"

Sage Chicken

Chicken pieces, cut up for frying (up to two whole
    chickens can be used)
2 cans cream of mushroom soup (low-fat, low-
    sodium is fine)
1 soup can water
1 tablespoon rubbed sage
Salt and pepper to taste
Prepared rice, noodles, or mashed potatoes

In a large pot, brown chicken pieces in as small
an amount of cooking oil as you can get away with
using. Add soup, water, sage, and salt and pepper to
taste. Stir. Cover and cook over medium heat for
about 40 minutes, turning occasionally, until the
chicken is done and the sauce is like gravy. Use sauce
as gravy for rice, noodles, or mashed potatoes.

BLENDER FLAN

½ cup sugar

8 eggs

2 cans evaporated milk

¾ cup sugar

2 teaspoons vanilla

Caramelize sugar by melting it over low heat in a saucepan. Drizzle onto the bottom and sides of a round baking dish or individual custard cups, taking care not to give yourself third-degree burns in the process.

Put remaining ingredients in a blender and blend for about 15 seconds, or until the egg whites are no longer disgustingly visible. Pour into the baking dish.

Put the baking dish into a large pan that has a couple of inches of hot water in the bottom of it. Bake at 350 degrees F. until a knife inserted in the center comes out clean. This can take anywhere from 20 minutes or so, if you're using those cute little custard cups, to well over an hour if you're using a deep casserole dish. Chill.

To serve, loosen sides with a knife and invert onto a serving plate.

CLARK'S NIKUDANGO (JAPANESE MEATBALL) APPETIZERS

1 tablespoon finely chopped gingerroot

2 tablespoons chopped green onion tops

⅔ cup sugar

½ cup soy sauce

⅓ cup vinegar

3 tablespoons rice vinegar

¼ cup water

2 tablespoons cornstarch

2½ pounds meatballs, purchased or homemade*

Combine all ingredients except for meatballs in a frying pan. Stir over medium heat until dissolved and well mixed. Add meatballs. Mix well and cook for 30 minutes, stirring occasionally, until sauce has thickened and meatballs are warm.

*For homemade meatballs, combine the following: 2 pounds extra lean ground beef, 1 tablespoon finely chopped gingerroot, ½ cup cornstarch, ½ cup water, and ¾ teaspoon salt. Mix all ingredients till smooth, form into balls, and cook in hot oil over medium heat until brown on all sides.

A Joyful Tale

By Lael Littke

My dog, Harry, is blind. He smells a little because of a skin condition, and he's lost a lot of his hair for the same reason. He walks awkwardly because of arthritic hips. He is not an attractive dog.

But his ears flop forward and he peers somewhere in my direction when I speak to him. He smiles, or that's what his pleasant dog face appears to do. And he wags his tail eagerly, enthusiastically, even joyfully.

We used to call him the Joyful Dog. He didn't start off having much to be joyful about. He was found in a paper bag as a puppy, left on the lawn of an apartment house. One of the tenants found him. Noting that he had mange and a broken leg, she judged him useless and dumped him in a garbage can.

Fortunately she told the landlady, who went out and

found him deep in the garbage can, smiling up at her and wagging his tail. She gathered him up and gave him to a friend of mine who runs a dog rescue organization called Lifeline for Pets. My friend deposited him in the local kennel where she kept her rescued dogs while she sought homes for them.

That's where we found him after our ancient dog, Wilmer, died and we wanted to find another one who needed us.

We were shown several dogs, but it was Harry we chose, mainly because he came dancing out carrying his own leash. And wagging that joyful tail.

He wasn't all that attractive even then, a couple of years after he'd arrived at the kennel. Medium-sized, he looked like a cross between a German shepherd and a coyote, with coyote predominating. In fact, my friend told us she had despaired of ever finding a home for "that ugly dog."

But the "unwanted" were our specialty (at one time we shared our home with nine unwanted, abandoned, or mistreated cats), and we took him home. He carried his leash and wagged his tail all the way. He became a pleasant fixture around our house, never asking for anything, accepting whatever he got, whatever happened to him, with smiles and a wagging tail. He often got pushed aside by another, larger, abused dog we took in.

He's been with me now for eleven years, through earthquakes and high winds and flooding rain and fires that burned the mountains behind us (the four seasons in southern California). He kept us company when our daughter went away to college and marriage. He became my devoted companion after my husband, George, died of a sudden heart attack. It took him almost as long to stop listening for George's car as it did me. He was my security system, barking ferociously when anyone came onto my property.

Now he's old and smelly and blind. He spends most of his time resting on a small rug, dragging it around to wherever is warmest.

He still never asks for anything. Because of that I tend to neglect him.

Oh, I feed him regularly. I bathe him to keep his body odor in check. But I pay little attention to him as he sleeps in the sun.

One recent day I had to notice him because I stepped on him as he slept. Even though I hurt his paw, he wagged his tail.

Contrite, I knelt beside him, rubbing his pain-wracked body gently. I could tell how good it felt by his expression and the way he stumbled to his feet to follow me, whipping that joyful tail in circles, when I got up to leave. I rubbed him again, telling him how much I appreciated him and promising to rub him down more often. Then I searched out a long-forgotten dog biscuit recipe I had saved. After all, isn't food the universal comfort gift? If it works well for humans, wouldn't it work just as well for my dog, this uncomplaining "least of these"?

I felt that I was doing something good as I rolled out the dough, cut it, and put it in the oven. And

Harry, my humble, arthritic, blind friend, wagged his tail joyfully as I hand-fed him the warm biscuits. He understood that I loved him.

Dog Biscuits

2½ cups flour (preferably whole wheat)

½ cup nonfat dry powdered milk

1 teaspoon sugar

1 teaspoon salt

6 tablespoons margarine

1 egg

Mix ingredients with about ½ cup cold water. Knead for 3 minutes. Dough should form a ball. Roll to ½-inch thick and cut into dog bones. Bake on a lightly greased cookie sheet for 30 minutes at 350 degrees F.

Variations: Add powdered chicken or beef bouillon or dried soup mix.

GINGERBREAD MEN

BY ARDITH W. WALKER

Every Christmas our family's favorite tradition is to make gingerbread men to give for neighborhood gifts. Even though the gingerbread men are cut out with the same cutter, each one is just a little bit different. One will have his hand cocked up to the right, another his toe pointing down. Even the faces imprinted right in the dough never come out of the oven the same. I think maybe gingerbread men like to be different.

Unlike many of us. When I was in high school, the thing I wanted more than anything else was a Jantzen sweater. Everybody who was anybody had a Jantzen. I was obsessed with having a Jantzen. My parents couldn't afford to buy me one, so when I turned sixteen and got my first real job I immediately went out and bought a Jantzen. Then I bought another and another. Finally I belonged. Finally I was like everyone else. Finally I was popular. Then a new girl moved into our school, and we became good friends. I can remember how surprised I was when I realized that Pat didn't have any Jantzens. She was popular: a class officer, a school sweetheart, and in her senior year a cheerleader. She did all of that without one Jantzen sweater.

I liked the way my father didn't mind being different. He was probably one of the Church's most unusual bishops. Shortly after he became bishop in the 1940s, he was deluged with ward members' claims that this neighbor was committing adultery with that neighbor. So he stood at the pulpit and proceeded to forgive everyone—one giant blanket of forgiveness—and then told everyone to go home and sin no more.

During his term as bishop there were three old bachelors living in our ward named Oscar, Ike, and Jake. They drank whiskey and apparently didn't bathe much because I can still remember how they smelled, and I think I was only six at the time. Eventually Oscar and Ike died, and Jake couldn't take care of himself alone. So Daddy arranged to take him to a rest home. As Daddy was driving him to the rest home he said, "Jake, would you like one last glass of beer?" Jake said, "I sure would, Bishop." So my father the bishop stopped in front of Pleasant Grove Beer Hall, and Jake went in for one last glass of beer while Daddy waited for him in the car.

I like Daddy. I like Pat. I like gingerbread men. This Christmas—or if you really want to be different, maybe this July—make a batch of gingerbread men and watch them refuse to be exactly alike.

Gingerbread Men

1 cup margarine
1 cup sugar
1 cup dark molasses
3 eggs
6 cups sifted flour
1 teaspoon nutmeg
1 teaspoon baking soda
2 teaspoons baking powder
2 teaspoons ginger
2 teaspoons cloves
3 teaspoons cinnamon

Cream margarine and sugar. Add molasses and beat until fluffy. Add eggs and beat. Add remaining ingredients and mix well. Chill 1 hour. Roll out ¼-inch thick and cut out with cookie cutter. Bake on greased sheet 9 minutes at 350 degrees F. (It is better to underbake than overbake.) Makes approximately 2 dozen.

WHEAT MUSH AND MY GRANDFATHER'S NICKEL

BY EUGENE ENGLAND

My ninth birthday, July 22, 1942, was a bright, hot, early harvest day in Marsh Valley, southern Idaho. We lived on the northeast edge of the town of Downey and raised dryland wheat on 1,120 acres extending to the valley's eastern hills. Birthdays made little difference during harvest time. Our whole year's income came down to that five weeks of steady, sometimes frantic, work. We lived in constant worry that hail or wind or fire might take the rest of the crop.

So, even on my birthday I heard my father's forcefully cheery getting-up voice at the usual time, 5:00 A.M. I had my own room, which my father had excavated in the basement, next to the furnace and coal bin. In the winter I would first hear the motor of the automatic feeder start up and begin to run coal into the furnace with its metal worm. Then my father would call me from the head of the stairs where he had turned up the thermostat. But in summer there was only a fine stillness as I came softly from dreams. My dreams usually were not frightening but possessed of a total, sweet reality that I had no wish to leave. I could sometimes will myself to return to one for a while. That morning, feeling unusually alive and conscious of myself, I dressed quickly and went up to the kitchen at the first call. I was full of secret anticipation for the day.

Dad already had a fire going and cracked wheat cereal that had soaked overnight slowly boiling on the Monarch coal range. He said nothing about my birthday but served expertly while I crossed and hooked the rawhide laces up the sides of my boots. I tied them once, then pulled the extra length around the top of each boot and tied the laces tight enough to keep the wheat out when I shoveled in the truck or elevator bins. We knelt and prayed, my father as usual asking God to hold back the wind and hail and promising to use all the crop in His service. Then we poured on whole cream, risen in the bottles milked from our one cow, and scooped up blobs of dark clover honey in our spoons and let it melt slowly into the cream and wheat.

I slipped back downstairs for two of the red-and-yellow streaked, hybrid crab apples from my grandfather's tree that we had stored there just the week before. I grabbed my two new comic books and *The Black Arrow* and made it back just in time to jump on the running board and frantically swing inside the truck as Dad accelerated, laughing, out the driveway.

After we reached the field and Dad filled the large wooden bin on the truck with two loads of wheat from the smaller bin on our self-propelled harvester, I drove the truck to town. I picked up Bud Cranshaw, who drove the truck the rest of the day while I tended the small elevator by the railroad tracks where we stored the wheat until it could be sold at a higher price in the winter. I would turn on the machinery, and after Bud drove up a ramp and dumped the wheat in the elevator pit he would go back to the field for another load. I had to watch things carefully in case of breakdown or plug-up, keep the machinery oiled, and sometimes shovel the wheat away from the spout at the top of each bin, but most of the time I could read.

At six o'clock in the evening on my birthday, Bud came with Dad's present to me: word that I could ride home after the pit was empty, clean up, and go to the picture show while Dad and Bud finished up. I bathed and enjoyed a slow supper, then got the dime from my box and walked down the road that ran west, past Grandpa Hartvigsen's. I cut through the huge vacant lot to the main road running south through town, the other farmers' wheat trucks throwing out gravel as they sped past to the two main elevators.

The town's business section was clustered at a crossroads, three big clumps of stores and an implement dealer on the other corner, with a small movie theater in the largest clump. Movies were nine cents, which left a penny for a Tootsie Roll or all-day sucker or stick of Smith Brothers licorice. But that night I found that the price had gone up to fifteen cents for a special showing of *Abraham Lincoln.* Determined not to end my day with disappointment, I started running for home, but by the time I got to Grandpa's I knew I couldn't make it in time and ran into his kitchen exhausted and crying. He was a little, wiry, taciturn man, raised on a pioneer homestead in Utah by parents born above the Arctic Circle in Norway, and he didn't know what to do with me.

Finally he pulled out a big oval leather coin purse, with brass reinforcing along the top and three interlocking brass clips that would let him open one side or the other. He poured the coins into his hand, picked out a bright buffalo nickel for me, and motioned for me to follow him. Without a word, he led me out to his black, hump-backed 1939 Mercury, which he had bought to drive to the World's Fair in New York, and took me to the theater.

I got in after the previews but in time for the Movietone News. Footage about the Russian and British retreats and the bloody, continuing battle for Guadalcanal, and then the Bugs Bunny Cartoon, full of violence that never permanently hurt anyone. As I walked home in the dark, looking at the clouds of bright, close stars, I thought about Lincoln and soldiers dying, then about the black line marking the war fronts on the Movietone maps, steadily moving out from Japan and Germany. That night I dreamed there was a witch at the top of the stairs, her face red in the glow from the furnace door.

As I awoke in the dark the next day, I realized my father was standing by the bed, his hand still on my shoulder. "We need to get going," he said quietly. "Your grandpa wants to go with us today, so let's go help with his chores."

We ate and got down to Grandpa's by 5:00, in time for Dad to milk the last big black and white Holstein. Grandpa shoveled the manure from the floor and the little trench behind the four cows out the window onto the pile west of the milking shed, and I carried the six broad, three-gallon buckets, two at a time, up to the milk porch, walking very slowly so I spilled only a little. Then, while Grandpa fixed his breakfast, Dad poured one of the buckets into the top basin of the mechanical cream separator; I turned the crank, and the skim milk and cream shot out into pans from two separate jets. Dad poured the other buckets into a big ten-gallon can and set it out by the driveway to be picked up by the dairy truck, and then we had another bowl of cereal with Grandpa, using the fresh cream.

CRACKED WHEAT MUSH

(In memory of my father, who died in 1996 at the age of ninety-two)

1 cup cracked wheat (preferably cracked at
    medium setting of a hand-powered wheat
    grinder)
4 cups water
1 teaspoon salt (or to taste)

Soak wheat overnight for smoother texture and extra flavor, if desired, but this is not necessary.

Bring water and salt to brisk boil. *Slowly* pour in cracked wheat, so the boil continues and wheat does not form lumps. Lower heat to slow boil for ten minutes, stirring occasionally. Lower heat again, so *very* slow boil continues (only occasional plopping of bubbles to the top) for ten minutes or until ready to serve. Serve with honey and cream. Makes 4 servings.

WHOLE WHEAT MUSH

My grandfather's alternative is very good, though I don't like it as well. It has a soft, nutty flavor and a rubbery texture different from the cracked wheat Dad fixed. Using *whole* wheat, follow the same directions, but start in the evening and leave cooking on lowest setting overnight, or, immediately after the first slow boil, pour the cereal into a good thermos and leave it overnight.

A YEAR OF BEANS

By Natalie Curtis McCullough

The way the story came to me, I have to believe it. Even with its several family versions, it is a tale of unconscionable morbidity. But it is mostly true and bears retelling for the character it is bound to build in all of us.

It was the early 1930s, during the Great Depression. My mother was the youngest of nine hungry children. Times were tough. Grandpa did occasional carpentry work, but after they finished the road up Parley's Canyon with pick and shovel in the dead of winter, there was no more work to be found. Luckily, a fire burned down the back room of Keeleys Ice Cream Parlour and Diner, and Grandpa was hired to clean up and rebuild it. He took his son, Lee, to help him.

Grandpa and Grandma had been able to buy a

hundred pounds of beans and a hundred pounds of wheat during the last job. People all over the country were hungry. They were standing in soup lines. So, actually, the Romneys were fortunate. Grandma sent children to the store for "a nickel's worth of hamburger" to flavor the beans for her family of eleven. Apparently even the butcher was incredulous and asked aloud just what anybody could do with a nickel's worth of hamburger, not to mention a family of *eleven*. Nevertheless, the family survived for more than a year on home-baked wheat bread and beans "flavored with hamburger." Bread and beans. Every day. One year of beans is a lot of days.

Now, the older boys could work odd jobs for a few extra dimes here and there. It got them to the ward show on Friday nights. It bought them a bag of corn to pop for a party. It helped in a crisis. But really, the crisis was an ongoing, everyday monotony of survival on wheat and beans. For the most part, all paychecks were turned over to Grandma.

Given this backdrop, you will agree that Uncle Lee's behavior was completely spectacular. He got paid small wages for his work at Keeleys. One night after work he walked in the front door and told Grandpa to get his hat and coat, they were going out to dinner.

Grandpa had to get up from the dinner table. The faces around it looked to him in awe. Their father and one of their brothers, Lee, could walk away from the crowded little kitchen with its smells of baking bread and simmering beans. Walk away from the pleasant banter and argument, the gossip and accounting of a day's activities. They could leave the joking and jostling for attention. If two of the family left, Grandma would have a place to sit down—if she decided she wanted to after so many years proclaiming her satisfaction with standing by the stove, one foot resting on the warm lip around the bottom. Afton might not have to perch on the broken stool, but could take a chair with a back. With two gone, every son's shoulders might square to the table. Think of that. The smells continued, the cracked linoleum remained the same, the fogged window dripped occasionally, but the familiar sounds of family silenced, for a moment, while Grandpa rose from his place at the head of the table. His bread uneaten, his bowl of beans barely touched, he put down his fork and went for his hat.

Some of the daughters were biting their tongues against the injustice. They worked hard too, after all. Why didn't washing and ironing and scrubbing old floors pay dimes toward a diner for them? Aunt Bea even had a full-time job at the Presiding Bishop's office, but after she paid $6.60 in tithing and kept $2.30 for nylons, the rest of her monthly paycheck was turned over to the family. In fact, for many months, she had been the only wage earner in the family. Nevertheless, it was Grandpa and Lee who were going to Keeleys. My mother, about five years old, smiled up at Grandpa. Perhaps when you are the youngest, you learn to expect that good fortune has a longer path to your door. You learn to be happy for the person so far away from you in the front of the line. Her father paused at her chair. She was his little Ladybird. He squeezed her shoulder with his rough hands before he strode out the door without a backward glance.

Grandma didn't even begrudge it. To think that her husband and son were going to the diner to eat. It was impossible! Imagine eating meat loaf, roast beef and potatoes with gravy, fried chicken and carrots, split pea soup! She would not have been able to choose even if she got the chance. Go, she thought, I am content to dream of it.

Lee had been saving his money with this great moment in mind, and now it had come. It was about more than food. This was his proclamation of manhood. It was his rite of passage into an independent life not necessarily dictated by the demands of so many children. They were a father and son, stepping out to the diner for a bite to eat and man's talk that didn't center on where work could be found or whose clothes were beyond mending or whether the country could ever recover its economic base. This was the honest-to-goodness feel of normalcy. They walked down the street together, proud against the cold. Here was real life to tide them through the fog of unreality they worked and slept through day after day. Two men going to the diner. Just once, in the empty vacuum of that year, something different to eat. Something different to eat! They walked side by side down the dusk of that sidewalk. Neither of them owned gloves, but that night it did not matter. I believe that my grandpa was thinking about gravy.

They weren't gone all that long. Grandma was waiting, wanting to hear every buttery detail. She may have been kneading in a drop of food coloring to make a pound of milky lard pass as butter for her family. Suddenly there were boots on the front porch. That was odd; she had not heard voices. Voices usually seemed to carry from a ways down the street. Then the two of them came through the front door. It seemed to her that they were not all that euphoric. They walked in the house, nodded to each other, put their wraps in the closet. Lee looked at Grandma for a moment, the expectation in her eyes breaking his heart, and then he looked down, passing her to go to his studies. Grandpa sat in the front room with the paper. But Grandma was not to be denied.

"Well, what did you order?" She was all anticipation, her hands clutching her apron, her eyes shimmering in the lamplight. Her mind fluttered on sparrow's wings with the possibilities she had allowed herself to imagine.

"A bowl of beans," came the reply without a trace of emotion. In fact, without so much as a lifting of his eyes from the paper.

"Beans?" my grandmother asked, wounded, deflated, stupefied. And then again, as if to let it register, this grand moment of triumph shattered by the hateful word, "beans?" He was kidding, of course, that old stinker! And yet there was the silent entry, the way

Lee had looked away from her, her husband's odd fixation on the newspaper—all of it old news anyway—as confirmation. They had gone to the diner and eaten beans.

She wandered back to the kitchen. Puttered there awhile, absently put beans in the big old pot to soak overnight. Then back to the living room she went, though not to sit, only to put her head in and ask in the most shaken of voices, "Father, why beans?"

Grandpa lowered the newspaper, barely. He took several deliberate, deep breaths before saying, "When the waitress asked for our order, Lee couldn't think what to say. So he ordered us two bowls of beans." He paused a long time, then continued, "After the waitress left, I asked why he ordered beans. Lee said he was very hungry and beans were the most food you could get for ten cents." Another pause before he looked up. "Good night, Mother." But he didn't move to walk upstairs. It only meant that he was tired now. The momentous event was over and there was nothing else to say about it.

Grandma pondered this. Roast beef, chicken, split pea soup . . . a dish of ice cream and he couldn't think what to say? The sinful waste! Couldn't think what to say. Wasn't a meat pie only fifteen cents? It was no use knowing now. So her boy had left the drudgery of her table for the big diner, for his own chair with nobody crowding him at his elbow and a menu with choices. When he got there, the tidal pull of the familiar proved too great, too safe, too much. He ordered two bowls of beans.

Grandma tossed a dish towel over her shoulder and prepared to wash the soaking dishes. Oddly enough, she felt like giggling. She wanted to toss her head and twirl, as if the desire to dance were a great pressure backed up inside her. Fishing for the washrag, she smiled into the dirty dishwater alone in the glow of her dimly lit kitchen. It was forgivable after all, more bowls of beans.

NANA ROMNEY'S SURVIVAL BEANS

Soak 1 pound red beans all night in 2 quarts water. Throw water away and replace fresh in the morning. Simmer several hours. Or, simmer beans all day on coal stove. Pour in one quart jar of home-canned tomatoes. Flavor with a nickel's worth of hamburger, fried. Salt down. Add chili powder to taste. Add chopped onion, pressed garlic, or tomato sauce for variety. Enjoy with homemade whole-wheat bread. (If possible, eat sparingly.)

MOTHER-IN-LAW WILMA'S BETTER BAKED BEANS

1 large can B&M baked beans, undrained
2 medium cans red kidney beans, drained
2 cans lima beans, drained, or 2 packages frozen
    lima beans, thawed
1 medium onion, chopped
3 cloves garlic, minced
1 teaspoon dry mustard
½ cup brown sugar (or more to taste)
1 cup catsup (or more to taste)
¼ teaspoon pepper
½ teaspoon salt
½ pound bacon, fried crisp and crumbled
1 small can crushed pineapple, undrained
    (optional)

Combine all beans in large casserole dish. Sauté onion and garlic until tender; add remaining ingredients. Add to beans and bake at 350 degrees F. until warmed through, about 45 minutes.

BAKED OXFORDS
À LA FRANÇAISE

BY ELOUISE BELL

Sister Anne Dudleston didn't know much about missions before she arrived in France in the spring of 1961. A convert, with no family in the Church and in fact with very little family at all, she simply had a powerful testimony and a genuine desire to serve. So she sold her car to finance her mission, left the University of Wyoming and the members of the Church she knew there, and said good-bye to her brother in Illinois. Anne's father had died when she was six; her mother had passed away a week after her daughter's high school graduation. No one waved good-bye to the twenty-one-year-old missionary when, after the three-day orientation, she flew out of Salt Lake City, headed for Paris with the other greenies in her group.

She was so unfamiliar with the nature of mission life that when a few of us from the mission staff greeted the newbies at the Orly airport, she thought the second counselor was my husband. I quickly explained that I was just another missionary, as was Elder Dodd, who politely looked the other way during my explanations.

Sister Dudleston also had not reckoned with the great amount of walking missionaries did. (Actually, she didn't know exactly *what* missionaries did. Had she known, the shy Sister D. might well have stayed in Laramie!) The shoes she had brought were inadequate, so she wrote her brother to send a pair of sturdy oxfords. (No French store could fit her long, narrow feet.) And she waited many weeks before the package came.

The shoes arrived on a rainy fall day. Sister Dudleston put them on—they fit beautifully—and joined her district in a trip to the mission home for brochures and supplies. I was secretary to the mission president at the time, and, with the rest of the mission staff, I lived in the headquarters in Paris's elegant 16th quarter. When Sister Dudleston squished wetly in through the great door of the mission home, I was appalled. She looked every bit as bedraggled as the poor unfortunates who congregated in the Metro (subway) entrances. Her thin raincoat was not behaving as raincoats should behave, her ungloved hands were blue with cold, and her new shoes were already sopping. Something had to be done!

I took her to the sister missionaries' room, hung up her pathetic raincoat, gave her a towel for her hair, and wondered what to do with her shoes, heavy with rainwater. They needed to dry—and in a hurry. Well, what's good for the goose must be good for the oxfords, I thought. So I stuck her shoes in the kitchen oven, set the temperature at medium, and returned to the sisters' room to see how she was faring.

New missionaries are always in need of a listening ear. They have stories to recount that you just can't believe! (You neglect to tell them how many times the previous week you have heard the same sort of tale.) So I listened as Sister Dudleston outlined the terrors, disappointments, and surprising joys of her recent days. I clucked, consoled, nodded, and tried to encourage. And also, at last, I sniffed. A distinctly unsavory smell was wafting from the kitchen.

THE SHOES! They were dry, all right. But another mighty change had been wrought. What had been size 8 oxfords were now curled and wizened size 4s. The new shoes had shrunk beyond recognition.

No need to describe the next hour. Sister Dudleston hobbled from the mission home in a pair of my tracting shoes, definitely not a happy substitute for the baked oxfords. I wondered if she would ever forgive me.

She must have done so, for we became lifetime friends. When, a few months later, she broke both knees in a motor scooter accident, I visited her daily in the American Hospital at Neuilly and kept her spirits up by pinching her bare toes, exposed as she lay in traction. When she finished her mission (a little thing like two broken knees only slowing her down, never stopping her), she came to BYU, and we roomed together for the next nine years.

In the course of time, Anne married the boy next door, earned a Ph.D. in Food Science and Nutrition, and had four children. After her marriage we remained close. Her children consider me their aunt, and I delight in their soccer wins, report cards, rock-climbing exploits, and mission calls. Anne is an uncommonly good cook, ranking high among the fabled food wizards of Mormondom, and I have enjoyed many a fine Sunday dinner at her table. Wonderful dishes come from her oven, but none has given us as many laughs, in retrospect, as has *my* specialty—Baked Oxfords à la Française!

ANNE'S POTATO CASSEROLE

This potato casserole is a simple one, and simply marvelous. Recently, a husky young firefighter, a guest at Anne's table, tasted the dish and grew wide-eyed. "If you brought that to the fire station," he attested, "it would disappear in sixty seconds flat!"

8 or 9 medium potatoes, boiled in jackets, THEN
    peeled and diced
12 tablespoons melted butter
6 tablespoons chopped green onions
2 cans cream of chicken soup, undiluted
1 pint sour cream
½ cup milk
2 cups grated cheddar cheese
2 cups crushed cornflakes

Grease a 9 x 13-inch baking dish. Place diced potatoes in the dish. Drizzle 6 tablespoons of the melted butter over potatoes. Sprinkle onions evenly over potatoes. Mix soup, sour cream, and milk. Pour mixture over potatoes. Sprinkle grated cheese over this mixture. Cover evenly with crushed cornflakes. Drizzle remaining 6 tablespoons melted butter over the casserole. Bake at 350 degrees F. for 35 to 40 minutes.

THE TEETOTALING* FIASCO

BY RICHARD H. CRACROFT

There we were, in early February 1959, two recently released Mormon missionaries being driven from Brighton on the English Channel to Worthing, in company with a dapper but elderly Oxonian and London business owner and his bright, vivacious, and oh-so-British wife. We were winding through the faded green downs of southern England in a mint-condition 1935 automobile toward what we would discover to be a charming, 300-year-old home complete with thatched roof and oft-encountered ghost. (The ghost was a

---

*Of or pertaining to, advocating, or pledged to total abstinence from intoxicating drink; reduplicated variant of "total," coined by R. Turner, of Preston, England, in 1833, in a speech advocating total abstinence from alcoholic drinks.

pleasant old sea captain who delighted family members but nonplussed guests by entering the two-story home through the back door, looking in on what was going on, nodding pleasantly, and hobbling up the stairs—the Thompsons even had photographs!)

Guided to this gracious and intelligent couple by my Salt Lake City aunts, one of whom was a native-born Brit, I was delighted by the cordial welcome from these unknown cousins. My traveling companion and I were both impressed that I had such obviously cultivated and prosperous relatives, and in my youthful and heady vanity—and a bit intimidated by their British ways and speech—I was eager to make a favorable impression on the Thompsons.

Elder Paul Cannon Pollei, my friend since kindergarten, had been released on January 14 from his mission to Paris, France. After meeting at my Swiss-Austrian Mission headquarters in Basel, Switzerland, we had embarked on a month-long tour of Italy, Switzerland, Austria, Germany, France, Belgium, and Great Britain. We had made our way across Europe—debonair, cosmopolitan sophisticates, or so we imagined, fluent as we were in German and French, and both of us lovers of grand opera and art. Paul's piano keyboard wizardry had paid for our bed and board in a dozen homes of Latter-day Saints across Europe, most of which had some sort of piano in need of a performer. As Paul performed his repertoire to the admiration of all, I would sit, smile, contribute an occasional remark, and try to look like a connoisseur of the arts—or drop into profound slumber.

So I was counting on Paul to dazzle my cousins during the coming evening. They would be impressed by his cultivated gift and sophisticated ways. Aware that the Thompsons had unwittingly opened their home and their lives to a pair of twenty-two-year-old strangers from the American Wild West ("say *al-yu-min-i-yum* again for us," they would chuckle on hearing our pronunciation of *aluminum*), I was very conscious of the fact that we had not yet had opportunity to explain that we were (aha!) Mormon missionaries—wolves in American sheep's clothing.

Enjoying the quaint country roads on that grey and wintry afternoon, we entered a small village. Our genial host turned in his seat, pointed to an ancient building on the right, and said, "I say, lads, I know how you Americans enjoy your spot of whiskey; there's a lovely old pub right here where we can enjoy a drop."

The moment of revelation was upon us: the poor, wayfaring strangers would now have to start from disguise and stand up for the Restored Gospel—suavely, of course. Sitting forward in the backseat, I edged into First Discussion position and said, like the world-traveled, veteran Elder of Israel I most surely was, "What you have on your hands, dear cousins, are two Mormon missionaries who are returning to Utah after thirty months in service to our faith."

I paused, assessing the damage to that point, and then continued. "As you may know, it is a tenet of our faith that we don't use tobacco or drink any kind of alcohol. We would love to go into the pub with you, but you need to know that Paul and I are both strict *teetotalers*," I added, pleased that I could use that word so exactly in such a situation. I relaxed a bit, the revelation made, and ignored the little slumping of our hosts' shoulders.

But Elder Pollei could not let my perceived treachery go unchallenged. As if jabbed by a bayonet, Paul came to attention in the seat next to me. Glaring icicled daggers at me, his erstwhile and suddenly traitorous companion, he spat out his words in a Samuel-on-the-walls-of-Zarahemla voice: "We are NOT teetotalers. At least," he glared at me again, "*I* am not a teetotaler." Then, his Charlton-Heston-voiced clincher: "I have never had a cup of tea in all my life."

Then silence.

"I see," saith our goodly host after long seconds, his eyes and his wife's eyes wide open and eyebrows arched, as if to say, "There goes the weekend, luv."

We drove by the pub. I attempted to conceal my dismay at Paul's blatant shattering of our cosmopolitan facade by defining "teetotaler" for my still irate companion. We arrived at the Thompsons' thatched cottage and made ourselves at home. Famished, we stuffed ourselves at their suddenly tealess five o'clock tea, which we ravenous cosmopolites thought was supper. Forty minutes later, to our chagrin, we were invited to sit up to a several-course meal, where we amused my cousins with our Wild West appetites.

We were treated graciously but somewhat warily by the couple, who, fearful of our next move, told us that, by the way, they were quite happy with their lifelong religion. They chatted about the family ghost, themselves, and family, and inquired about their American cousins. Watching for the right moment, I seized opportunity to introduce Paul's talent, eager as I was to burnish our tarnished images. Equally eager to repair the "teetotaler" fiasco, Paul launched into his surefire concert of nine or ten numbers.

I was just beginning to relax when the couple, applauding Paul's second solo, stood up, thanked him, noted that it was already nine o'clock, wished the astonished, tea-totaling teetotalers good night, and consigned me to a tiny bedroom at the turn of the stairs. Made slightly ill at ease by tales of the ghostly sea captain, I turned on the light and found myself reading the witches' scene in *Macbeth,* which made me even more uneasy. I turned to prayer and then, to divert my attention from the sounds on the stairway, concentrated my thoughts on my imminent reunion with family and friends who knew me for the common-taters I was (and so remain) in beloved, unpretentious, and, yes, teetotaling Utah.

Swiss Birchermuesli

Birchermuesli, the Swiss national dish, is enjoyed in all families and served in every restaurant in Switzerland. The nutritionally "perfect" meal, created in 1897 by pioneering nutritionist Dr. R. Bircher-Benner, *Birchermuesli* continues to be served at every meal to patients at the Bircher-Benner Clinic in Zurich (one block down the street from the Switzerland-Zurich LDS Mission Home). Generally served with whole wheat or other dark breads and butter, the delicious dish also goes well with muffins and sweet rolls. Janice and I often serve the *muesli* at breakfast or supper or as the featured refreshment at social gatherings. I first enjoyed *Birchermuesli* in July 1956, as a fresh-off-the-boat LDS missionary in Linz, Austria. My companion, Elder Gary O'Brien, told me, mysteriously, to put an apple in my satchel "for later." That evening, the eight missionaries gathered in the branch house kitchen, extracted various fruits, sacks of nuts, and jars of yogurt from their briefcases, and watched as Elder Oswald Schwemmer combined our various offerings into a delicious, refreshing, and wonderfully nutritious *muesli,* which our family, responding to Janice's own touches, has enjoyed ever since.

1 large carton flavored yogurt

2 tablespoons lemon juice

1 large peeled apple, grated or diced

½ cup raisins

½ cup slivered almonds or chopped nuts

2 bananas, sliced

Fruits as desired in any combination: oranges,

mandarin oranges, berries, fruit cocktail
(drained)

¼ to ½ cup dry quick-cooking (not instant) oatmeal

Mix all ingredients, adding oatmeal gradually
until the *muesli* reaches a thick, creamy consistency.
(Flavored yogurt sweetens sufficiently; Bircher-
Benner's recipe calls for sweetened or honied con-
densed milk instead, but yogurt is much better!)
Chill for about 1 hour to allow flavors to blend.

Partake, emitting spontaneous, Alp-echoing,
yodeled yelps of joy (also good for the lungs, chest,
and sense of well-being). Serves 4 to 6.

Feijoada (American Style)

By Orson Scott Card

I delayed my missionary service for a year, and one of the main reasons was my fear of the food. I had a testimony, I hoped to serve a foreign-language mission, I wanted to immerse myself in another culture—except at mealtimes.

Fussy eating was a family tradition, but I was at the extreme. For instance, I hated strawberries. Mind you, I had never actually eaten a strawberry. But I knew I would hate them because they were bumpy. I couldn't eat Jello because if I got any of that thicker scummy stuff in my mouth I would gag. Pudding was out—like Jello it was a mouth-feel thing. There was no vegetable that I would eat except corn and peas. Green salads bored me; fruit salads were fine as long as the fruits were bananas, apples, and mandarin oranges. Anything more exotic than that—and I mean pears, peaches, grapes, or those nasty little marshmallows people put in salads in Utah—and I wouldn't touch the salad. No pork of any kind (except well-done bacon). No macaroni, ever. No cheese except thin slices from a Kraft American brick. No cookies except snickerdoodles and chocolate chip cookies—as made by my mother, my older sister, or me. And peanut butter and jelly? Gross.

Those who have raised fussy-eater children can hardly be surprised by my list—it isn't even restrictive, compared to one fussy eater I know who for ten years would order nothing in any restaurant except for plain pasta with Parmesan cheese. The only real surprise is: How in the world did I get to be overweight, when I wouldn't eat anything? The answer is that of those few things I did eat, I ate copiously.

The worst thing to place before me was . . . anything strange, new, exotic. And, by definition, that's what they serve on foreign missions.

Of all strange and exotic foods I feared, the most forbidding were the foods of the Orient. Chinese food, Japanese food, Thai, Filipino, Indian cooking—I knew that if I went on a mission where any of those cuisines were served, I would probably die before I reached my three-month mark (based on a rough estimate of how long my body fat would last me).

So when I finally worked up the courage to send in my papers, and my mission call came, I was deeply relieved that it was not to an oriental country. Brazil Central Mission, the letter said. That was in South America. It had "America" in the name, so it couldn't be too strange, could it? Besides, I liked tacos and burritos, and those were Mexican foods, and Mexico was part of Latin America, so I'd do fine, wouldn't I?

During my time in the LTM, I was frightened and lonely, and the mashed-potatoes-gravy-and-bread cuisine was my primary comfort. I gained weight until, by the time I left, I weighed in at 225 pounds. My suits were tight. My face was so puffy that it took me three seconds to shave instead of my usual two. But I think that I was putting on the weight by instinct: I knew I was heading to a land without edible food, and I had to build up my reserves.

In Brazil, my worst fears were quickly realized. We were given a lecture about what not to eat: no fruits or vegetables that we didn't peel ourselves—and lettuce was out, period. (Vital Portuguese phrase: *Sem alface,* meaning "without lettuce.") No water, ever. And when we drank pop it had to be from bottles, and our lips could touch only the portion of the bottle that had been heat sealed under the cap.

Yeah, that was just what a food-paranoid like me needed to hear.

Then I found out what Brazilians actually eat. Beans! Rice! I might as well have gone to Korea. I had never met a bean I could stand to eat. My mother had tried to serve them now and then—having been raised in the Depression, she felt there was something virtuous about eating lima beans and navy beans and all the other hideous, sickly beans that tasted like sticky dust in my mouth. As for the rice, it wasn't good, honest Minute Rice with butter or gravy on it. It was clumpy and bland, and the only thing they put on it was—you guessed it—beans.

And the most hideous imaginable food was the national dish: a black bean stew called Feijoada. Longtime missionaries loved to goad greenies like me by telling us how gross Feijoada was, how they put in it all the most disgusting parts of the pig. What they didn't realize was that it was enough for me to know that it had black beans and sausage in it. Once that was known, they could put roadkill in it, asphalt and all, and it wouldn't make any difference to me, because I was never going to eat it.

My first month in Brazil, all I ate—and I mean all—was bananas and grape Fanta. The other elders in Araraquara watched me with some amusement as I turned down the beans and rice with which they covered their plates. I wouldn't even eat the bread because it was crusty instead of being nice soft-crusted American bread.

Eating nothing but bananas eventually does things to your body that are not appropriate to describe in a book designed to make people hungry. Suffice it to say that after a month I knew I had to get some variety in my diet. And, bit by bit, I began to let my horizons widen. A little.

At first it was peanut butter. I had never actually

tried peanut butter back in the States—like strawberries, peanut butter looked disgusting enough that I hadn't felt the need to taste it. Now it became my lifeline: a thin coating of peanut butter made the strange bread palatable.

The missionaries in Araraquara had the habit of going down to the railroad station and eating P-Day Eve dinner at the restaurant there. I broke down and ordered a steak with ham and peas in a butter sauce. I had never liked steak, I didn't like ham, and peas were merely tolerable. But to my surprise, Brazilian steak wasn't like American steak. It was tender, flavorful, delicious. And the sauce with the peas and ham was amazing. For the first time it dawned on me that maybe there were Brazilian foods that were *better* than anything in America. Steak was one of them.

Gradually I began to try more and more Brazilian food. Guaraná, the most wonderful soft drink. Orange juice—Americans don't even know what orange juice is. Brazilian *pão doce,* a sweet pastry that has no American or European equivalent—even though you had to watch carefully to keep bees from getting in your sack of *pão doce,* it was worth the risk of getting stung.

The list goes on. Brazilian chocolates made the American version seem waxy and flavorless. Brazilian papayas are the size of watermelons, and, sweetened with Brazilian sugar (much less refined than American sugar, so you can pile it on for texture as well as flavor), they're delicious. At the time of my mission, *vitamina* drinks were all the rage—papaya, fresh pineapple, bananas, and either milk or orange juice, all blended together with enough ice to make the drink cold.

Brazilian ice cream (*sorvete*) was exquisite, especially pistachio. Not till I ate French *glace* and Italian *gelato* did I find anything comparable. (The only place in America to get that quality is in Santa Monica, at a little Austrian ice cream place, Charlie Temmel's, a few doors down from Barnes & Noble on the Third Street Promenade. Try the pistachio. That's the ice cream they serve in the celestial kingdom, I promise.)

During the first six months of my mission, I lost forty pounds and had a tailor take in my suits so the pants didn't fall off. But halfway through my mission, I realized I was putting the weight back on, because I had discovered that one of the most delicious dishes ever created was: beans and rice. Brazilians don't use those nasty, flavorless white beans that American culinary torturers force on us. No, the beans we had were dark and rich and flavorful, and the best beans of all were the dark-purple ones called "black beans." When I went to a restaurant to eat that perfect steak, I piled up the beans and rice—and took plentiful helpings of *farofa,* a powdery side dish made of ground-up manioc root with spices and bits of ham and vegetables.

I loved Brazil, you see. The food was only the outward symptom. I loved the people. I loved the language. I loved the noisy cities, the crazy traffic; I loved the countryside, the smaller towns, the shops, the houses with their walled gardens. I loved clapping my hands out on the street instead of knocking right on the door. I loved the polished tiles on walls, floors, ceilings—in colors and designs that clashed (to American eyes) but soon made sense (as my eyes became more Brazilian). I loved the graciousness with which we were taken into people's homes. I loved the buses and trains, the cobblestones and tiled sidewalks that were washed by householders every morning. I loved the kids who could keep a soccer ball in the air using only their feet for ten, twenty, fifty kicks. I loved the music—"MPB," the *musica popular brasileira,* which was heard commercially from artists like Caetano Veloso, Chico Buarque, Milton Nascimento, Maria Bethânia, Gilberto Gil, and many others; but which was most delicious when you heard it on the street, emanating from every corner bar/convenience store, where ordinary people would play intricate, impossible rhythms using the silverware, their bodies, and other implements in the bar. I loved the exuberant samba, that festive dancing that the Brazilians call "jumping" because that's how natural a part of their lives it is. I loved the way the gospel entered the lives of these people and brought out the best in them without taking away any of the most wonderful aspects of their culture. They took me into their homes and hearts, and as I walked those streets I felt that I was home.

But I was getting fat again.

I controlled myself. I dieted. I got off the bus before my stop and briskly walked the extra distance to get more exercise. (Elder Lima, my patient companion, endured this without complaint.) When I went home, I was two inches taller than when I had left (genetics did that) and weighed 176 pounds, the least I had weighed in my adult life. My mother thought I must have hated the food, because I was so thin. Quite the contrary. It took a long time to get used to American cooking again. It always seemed that something was missing.

Which brings us to the recipe I'm about to give you. I've served my version of Feijoada to a Brazilian, and although he liked it, he candidly told me that no *way* was it really Feijoada. Why? Because I couldn't get the right meat and spices. But that's all right. They really do use parts of the pig that I prefer not to serve; and as for the dried beef, I think the eye of round or London broil my recipe calls for is a better-than-fair substitute. The thing that's missing is the sausage. But I can't help that. As far as I know, you can't *get* that spicy sausage in America. And most Americans aren't in love with the peppers anyway.

So my Feijoada isn't authentic. But the black beans are still the food of kings, and as long as you don't use Minute Rice but instead use thick, clumpy *real* rice, you'll have a delicious meal, exotic enough to appall the fussy eaters in your family but delicious enough to make converts of at least a few of them.

Of course, you have to be able to pronounce it. If you remember a little high school Spanish, *forget it at once.* Portuguese is not Spanish. The *J* is not pronounced like an *H.* Instead, the *J* is pronounced like the second *G* in *garage,* or like the *Z* in *azure.* (And if you aren't pronouncing those two the same, you're not pronouncing *garage* correctly. Isn't it wonderful how many useful things you learn while reading cookbooks?) So *Feijoada* is pronounced: fay-ZHWAH-dah. But if that's still too hard, do as my young nieces did and just pronounce it "fishwater." It's not a terribly appetizing idea, but the sound is close enough. . . .

And if you want to have a real treat, serve your salad in the form of *vitaminas*. In a regular blender, put a cut-up (and cored) apple, a short can of pineapple, a cup or so of orange juice, and a banana or two. Also, put in some papaya—even those scrawny California or Sonora papayas will add the flavor and consistency. If you can't get papaya, or are too put off by the black caviar-like seeds (which you *remove* and throw away!), a quarter of a cantaloupe is a good substitute. Drop a couple of ice cubes into the blender and frappé the mixture. You should end up with a thick, delicious drink. And once you have that experience, try different variations. The most popular way to drink it in Brazil was with milk instead of orange juice, and many missionaries loved it with half an avocado added. A handful of strawberries or raspberries or blueberries blended in at the end make a wonderful variation. Far better (and better for you) than a milkshake.

As for the Feijoada, if you like my American version but still want to try the real thing, I know of two restaurants that serve it. In my hometown of Greensboro, North Carolina, the Leblon Brazilian Restaurant serves Feijoada two days a week—but they use such a mild sausage (so as not to scare off American eaters) that you're still not getting the real experience. In Washington, D. C., however, try the Amazonia Grill on Wisconsin. Their Feijoada is much more authentic, and very delicious—though you have to be ready to remove a few odd bones, usually from your mouth, since they're hard to spot in the stew. Don't try to guess what part of the pig they come from.

Feijoada (American Style)

Rinse 2 cups black beans in cold water. Place in crock pot with 5 cups cold water. Remove all floating beans and debris. Soak beans for 10 to 12 hours. Do not drain water. Add:

½ to 1 cup chopped leek or onion (to taste)

⅛ cup chopped fresh cilantro

1 can (16 ounces) stewed tomatoes (including juices); burst tomatoes with spoon so they don't stay whole during cooking

1 package powdered taco seasoning mix (Ortega)

1 to 2 teaspoons chili powder

2 to 3 teaspoons cinnamon

1 teaspoon lemon pepper

1 teaspoon tarragon

1 teaspoon garlic powder

3 dashes savory

3 dashes thyme

¼ teaspoon salt

½ an eye of round roast or ½ a London broil, diced to ½- to ¾-inch cubes (trim any fat)

Cook in crock pot on high 6 to 8 hours or on low 12 to 16 hours. One hour before end of cooking, add 1 can drained (cubed) mandarin oranges. Serve over rice.

Optional: top serving with cheese, chopped lettuce and tomato, and avocado.

Warning: juice of black beans will stain a permanent deep purple.

Apple Pie Baked in a Brown Bag

By Ardith W. Walker

When I was eighteen and still concerned about being beautiful, I was in a church play. During one of the practices a young man was brought into the auditorium in a wheelchair. I couldn't help noticing how he stared at me. He stared at me continually. He stared at me blatantly. He stared until I got so uncomfortable I felt his staring at me was the height of rudeness. After the practice we were introduced: he was blind.

A friend told me about apple pie that you bake inside a brown paper grocery bag. Stupid idea: for one thing, the bag would probably burn.

I hate to shop for shoes. I have fat toes and skinny heels, so I put it off as long as possible. But finally one

Saturday I worked up the courage to actually go shoe shopping. I went early to avoid any crowds. Thank goodness I was the only customer in the store. That way I could have the complete attention of the shoe salesman. I was relieved that the salesman was an older gentleman who would be knowledgeable and helpful. But he seemed uninterested in my fat toes and skinny heels. It was almost as if he weren't listening to me. He was not helpful. In fact, he was so distant I just about said something to him about it. As I got ready to leave, the phone rang. He grabbed the receiver and without even saying hello blurted, "Did they find her?" As I walked out, it sunk through my head that he had been worried about something more important than my fat toes.

Apple pie baked in a bag would taste like the brown paper bag, wouldn't it?

Some years ago my brother-in-law had his three-year-old son, Mark, with him in Salt Lake City. A homeless man walked by. He had long, stringy hair, a scraggly beard, and a dirty overcoat splotched with grease marks, and a cigar butt was hanging out of his mouth. Dennis tried to shield his son from seeing this derelict, but Mark noticed and said in awe, "There goes Jesus."

To make matters worse, the crust for the apple pie isn't even rolled out. You just pat it in the pie tin. Sounds like tough pie crust.

Growing up in Pleasant Grove, Utah, I went to school with the same eighty children from first grade through sixth grade. Those kids were like family. We knew each other and appreciated each other's strengths and weaknesses. Then in seventh grade about twenty new students from Lindon were bussed to our school. They were a strange and homely group. They all seemed a little slow. And not much fun. But somehow by eighth grade they got a lot more cute and smart and even witty. I wondered how they had managed to change so much.

I finally tried the apple pie baked in a bag. Now it's the only pie my family wants me to make.

Brown Bag Apple Pie

Crust:

1½ cups flour

2 tablespoons cold milk

½ cup salad oil

1 teaspoon salt

1½ teaspoons sugar

Combine all ingredients and mix until well blended. Pat into the bottom and sides of a pie pan. Do not roll.

Filling:

½ cup sugar

2 tablespoons flour

½ teaspoon nutmeg

½ teaspoon cinnamon

2 tablespoons lemon juice

7 cups Rome apples, sliced

Combine sugar, flour, nutmeg, and cinnamon. Toss lightly with lemon juice and apples. Put in unbaked shell.

Topping:

½ cup flour

½ cup butter

½ cup sugar

Combine all ingredients and mix with fingers until crumbly. Sprinkle on top of apples. Place pie in a brown paper bag, fold top over, and seal with a paper clip. Bake at 400 degrees F. for 1 hour. Don't peek!

MARTHA AND MARY AGAIN

BY ANN EDWARDS CANNON

I grew up in Zion's mountains, surrounded by Mormon women who had a certain fierceness born of competence. They could ride herd on a family bursting with children and keep them all clean, body and soul; they could till a deep backyard garden in the green of spring and can the fruits of their labors in the gold of fall; they could find shabby furniture at garage sales and refinish it so that it preened like new in the corner of the living room; they could, like Maria Von Trapp with an armload of curtains, subdue a formless stretch of fabric and turn it into a prom dress for their daughters.

They were Marthas, don't you know.

My own grandmother was the most Martha of

them all. When I returned home from living in Finland, her first question was, "How did you manage?" And then she was off with a barrage of related queries. What did I do for a bed? Where did I get linens, how much did they cost, and were they (she sincerely hoped) permanent press? Where did I buy my food? What was *that* like, and did I have to eat a lot of those fish—what were they called—herring? Did I have a fridge? And just how big were Finnish fridges these days, anyway?

I rolled my eyes straight back in my head. *I* wanted to talk about the sights that had stirred my twenty-something soul—birds hovering over seawater turned coppery rose by a midnight sun, green hay stacked for drying in fields that were greener still, heartbreakingly beautiful children whose skin was a seashell pink and hair a moonlit white. I wanted to take the things I had seen and turn them into words—poems, stories, books.

Unlike my grandmother, I was Mary.

I was Mary and that was okay. It was better than okay. In fact, I was Mary and that was better than being Martha. I knew this because I had read a liberating article that essentially gave women permission to be less than perfect on the domestic front by pointing out that it was Mary who had made the better choice, leaving the dishes in the sink and listening instead to the words of the Savior.

Naturally, I appreciated this perspective, because I *always* left dishes in the sink. I also did not sew or refinish furniture. I was not competent in the ways of so many of the Mormon women I had known, nor did I want to be.

Such was the arrogance of my youth.

Right now, as a forty-something female struggling to manage a household totaling seven people, I find the women I have begun to admire most are the ones, like my grandmother, who take an apron with them wherever they go, the ones who quietly do the work to finish up those dishes while everyone else listens. The ones who help. The ones who do. The ones who make things possible for other people. The ones who are gifted in the practical arts. The Marthas.

In my ward we have a Martha. Her name is Sharon and she is always there—at parties, dinners, wedding receptions, funerals, farewells. She arrives early and stays in the kitchen until everything is done. When I asked her once why she kept getting asked to do the cleanup, Sharon smiled and told me that she isn't always asked— she just shows up.

May the Lord bless her always.

Martha's Good Clam Chowder

I am fortunate to have a number of Marthas in my life—both figuratively and literally. This is my favorite soup recipe of all time, and it comes from a good friend named Martha Cooper.

¾ cup butter
5 tablespoons minced onion
¾ cup flour
6 cups half-and-half (this can be cut with regular milk)
1½ teaspoons salt
½ teaspoon pepper
2 cups diced potatoes
1 cup diced carrots
1 cup diced celery
½ cup water
4 cans (7 ounces each) chopped clams (save juice)

In a large kettle, melt butter. Add onion and sauté. Add flour and cook, stirring, until bubbly. Then add half-and-half, salt, and pepper. Cook over medium heat, stirring constantly, until thickened. Reserve.

Meanwhile, in another saucepan:

Cook diced vegetables until just tender in water and juice from clams. Stir into milk mixture. Add clams. Heat through. Serves 6.

LUCILLE
BAMBROUGH'S
CHOCOLATE CAKE

BY DONNA LEE BOWEN

When I was a Lark* in Primary, I decided that, as I would soon be a grown woman, I needed to get going on mastering womanly arts. I organized two other girls in my Lark class, Ann Chipman and Sheran Cheney, into our own cooking and sewing club. We met each week after school at one of our homes. One week we learned to cook something new; the next week we sewed potholders or embroidered dishcloths. As I stored

---

*Larks were young girls nine years of age. Larks marked the first year where girls and boys were segregated into separate classes, foreshadowing the future gender divisions to come.

each completed object in a tiny wooden chest, I was sure that working on these projects would ensure my readiness for marriage and family.

Ann's home was the best for cooking. Her mother, Sister Chipman, had lots of children and baked bread from scratch. She would bake loaves and loaves of bread a few times a week, and before baking the last loaf she would mix swirls of cinnamon, sugar, and chopped dates with the dough. If we headed to Chipmans' right after school, we usually arrived as the last loaf left the oven, and we could share in the treat.

Although Sister Chipman was the best bread baker, my mother was the best at baking sweets. She had many recipes inherited from her mother, my Grandmother Jenkins, who was not only a super cook but had gathered recipes from her Relief Society sisters, her Literary Club, and the Daughters of Utah Pioneers in both Ogden and Salt Lake City. She had lived in both cities for many years and served as Relief Society president (on both the ward and stake levels) in each place before moving across the street from us in Bountiful.

One week I begged my mother to allow me to bake the most elaborate chocolate cake recipe I knew of, the dense chocolate cake Mom made for birthdays and holidays: Lucille Bambrough's Chocolate Cake. Even the cadence of its name resonated with elegance, dignity, and adult concerns. Lucille Bambrough was a Daughter of Utah Pioneers colleague of my grandmother's in Ogden and the wife of Bishop Bambrough. Her prominence in Ogden society plus the excellence of the cake and the sophisticated cooking methods reflected in the recipe combined to impress me with Lucille Bambrough's high social status and excellent homemaking credentials.

Ann, Sheran, and I measured ingredients and began to assemble the cake. Melting chocolate in a double boiler was not difficult. Learning to separate eggs and beat the egg whites into a meringue was a new skill, but we leapt that rung with ease and proceeded to sifting flour and the dry ingredients. We had the egg yolks in a bowl ready to add with the wet ingredients, and the Wesson oil out ready to pour, when we came to a screeching halt. The recipe read "6 tblspns dry milk." "Dry milk"? we read questioningly. Why would Lucille Bambrough care whether the milk was dry or regular? What subtle taste difference did it make? We knew we did not like drinking dry milk, but somehow there must have been some mysterious, elusive flavor that only dry milk could impart to a chocolate cake. That ingredient must have been the reason that cake was so good. We carefully got down the red and white Carnation Powdered Milk package and read the instructions. Nowhere did it tell us how to mix a tablespoon of dry milk. We carefully measured six tablespoons of water into a cup, then attempted to calculate how much of a cup six tablespoons constituted. We decided that method needed higher mathematics than Larks had mastered, especially when something concrete depended on our math skills. We then reread the directions, figured out how to halve the recipe for one cup of dry milk, and measured and stirred. We then measured exactly six tablespoons of the newly mixed dry milk into our cake batter.

While the cake was baking, we asked my mother why Lucille Bambrough requested dry instead of regular milk. She looked puzzled; then she realized our mistake. She was tactful in breaking the news that it was the powder, not the liquid, that Lucille Bambrough was after. The cake smelled wonderful as it baked, but when we pulled it out of the oven, we realized that our interpretation of the dry milk had produced not Lucille Bambrough's Chocolate Cake, but Lucille Bambrough's Very Large, Flat, and Chewy Chocolate Brownie: the only brownie recipe extant that required separating the eggs and beating up a meringue.

When Lucille Bambrough consented to give Grandma a copy of her recipe, she made one condition. She extracted a promise that Grandma would never pass it on to anyone else. A woman of her word, Grandma did not. When she wanted to give my mother a copy, she telephoned Lucille and requested permission. Sister Bambrough since has passed away, but our family deference to her wishes lives on. I consulted my mother about publishing the Lucille Bambrough recipe. We discussed the matter and then agreed on a compromise: We will offer instead my grandmother's famous rich chocolate cake recipe, the one she made for birthdays and holidays, and keep Lucille Bambrough's Chocolate Cake recipe secret for her posterity.

CORA JENKINS'S CUSTARD CHOCOLATE CAKE

Custard:

4 squares unsweetened baking chocolate

1 cup brown sugar

½ cup milk

1 unbeaten egg

1½ teaspoons vanilla

Melt chocolate about halfway in top of double boiler over boiling water. Add brown sugar, milk, and egg, beating constantly with electric mixer, egg beater, or wire whisk. Continue beating over heat until mixture is thickened, glossy, and smooth. Remove from heat and stir in vanilla. Allow custard to cool.

Cake batter:

½ cup butter

1 cup sugar

2 eggs, beaten

1 cup milk

2 cups flour (measured after sifting)

½ salt

1 teaspoon soda dissolved in a little hot water

Cream butter with sugar. Beat eggs and add to creamed mixture with milk, sifted flour, salt, and dissolved soda. Fold cooled custard into batter. Pour into greased and floured 8- or 9-inch round cake pans or 13 x 9-inch dripper pan. Bake in 375 F. oven until cake springs back when touched gently in center, 20 to 25 minutes for round pans, 25 to 30 minutes for dripper pan.

COOKIES AND
COMFORT

BY LAEL LITTKE

"Come visit me," my friend Grace wrote from Las Vegas.

She had just lost her husband. I had lost mine four months earlier.

I decided to go. I envisioned us weeping together, two grieving widows recalling the years we'd shared in New York City when we were young and the future was an adventure. Those were the days.

I drove alone from Pasadena, recalling as I rolled along the freeway the many times George and I had driven through Las Vegas on our way to Salt Lake City without stopping to see Grace and Art. Now it was too late. Too late for George and Art, anyway.

But Grace and I would cry together and reconfirm to each other that the world was full of trouble and misery.

Grace had given me good directions, and I found her apartment easily. I dug out my Kleenex as I mounted the stairs, wadding a few tissues in my hand before ringing the doorbell.

Who would give out with the first wail of grief?

The door opened. "Hi," Grace said breathlessly. "Hurry and come in. I've got cookies baking." She turned and trotted toward the source of good smells.

I followed, holding back the tears that were standing at attention behind my eyes.

"Here," Grace said as I entered her kitchen. "Scoop the cookies off that tray."

I set down my purse and the wadded Kleenex. I scooped cookies onto a cooling rack.

She thrust a bowl and spoon at me. "Now fill it up again," she said. "A good teaspoonful for each cookie."

I did as she said.

When was she going to slow down so I could tell her how sorry I was about Art? When would she pause so we could clutch each other and cry?

By the time I'd filled up the cookie sheet again, there was another batch ready to scoop onto the cooling rack.

"There's no wheat flour in these cookies," Grace said as she shoved the newly filled sheet into the oven. "I bake them for a clinic for people who are allergic to wheat. Taste one."

The warm cookie was delicious. And comforting.

I had another one.

"Remember?" Grace said, and I got ready for the memories of George and Art to flow. But what she said was, "Remember those Manhattan Ward dinners we used to cook? And how George was always in charge of the turkeys?"

Here it was. We'd gotten around to George.

But I wasn't crying. I laughed as I remembered him stuffing all those naked birds on the very limited counter space in the cramped kitchen of the old church on 81st Street. He had an all-enveloping white apron, and sometimes he wore a chef's hat just for effect.

"He was so bossy," Grace said.

He was. We laughed together.

I felt better. "Grace," I said as I filled another empty cookie sheet. "This isn't what I expected we'd be doing." And I confessed how I'd thought we would just sit around and bemoan our fates.

"Not a chance," she said. "Read that."

She pointed to a small white card taped to her refrigerator. It said:

> Don't talk about your troubles
> And count them o'er and o'er,
> Or Heaven will think you like them
> And will send you more and more.

I had another cookie.

That visit was a turning point for me. I came home

cheerful and happy after my weekend with Grace, determined to get going on building my new life.

It hasn't all been easy. But whenever I fall into a pit, I take out the copy of the little white card that Grace gave me. No, I don't want "more and more." So I call up a friend to go to a movie, or I plan a trip, or I lose myself in the books I write.

Or sometimes I make cookies and take them to a friend who is downhearted.

KITCHEN SINK COOKIES

My favorite recipe is for a cookie redolent of good things, a fulsome comfort cookie that George called my "kitchen sink" recipe. I think of him and smile as I bake.

2 eggs

2 teaspoons vanilla

1 cup shortening

1 cup white sugar

1 cup brown sugar

1½ to 2 cups flour

1 teaspoon salt

1 teaspoon baking soda

2 cups oatmeal (old fashioned, not instant)

1 cup shredded coconut

1 cup chopped walnuts

1 cup chocolate chips

Preheat oven to 350 degrees F.

Beat eggs, vanilla, shortening, and sugars until well blended. Sift flour, salt, and baking soda. Stir into creamed mixture with remaining ingredients. Drop by teaspoonsful onto ungreased baking sheet, about 2 inches apart. Bake 10 to 12 minutes, until brown on edges but not dark. They are chewier if not too well done. Makes approximately 2 dozen.

COUNTRY ROOTS AND CITY SENSE

By Cathy Stokes

I admire women and men who bake bread. I admit I even covet that talent. Having failed to learn in more numerous attempts than I care to confess, I have looked for an alternative. What could I do that would taste homemade but not require more time than I have? Because I live in Chicago and commute 200 miles to the state capital every week, I don't have any spare time. And, because I have had my fill of failed attempts, what would be simple enough to be reliable every time? And if there were some historical/cultural/regional/ethnic significance, all the better.

Corn bread was a staple of my earliest childhood years in rural Mississippi. In fact, we had "white bread" only on limited occasions in the South and only for lunches after coming North. The most basic corn bread was hot-water corn bread, which consists of cornmeal with boiling water poured into it until it can be formed into patties. These patties are then fried in pork fat drippings. These days, more often than not, a corn-bread mix is used—and those with discriminating tastes can tell which brand.

Obviously corn bread was the right choice for me. Jiffy Corn Muffin Mix is frequently on sale, so that has become my preference. And, to make it feel more homemade, I figured out a way to doctor it up:

CORN BREAD

2 boxes Jiffy Corn Muffin Mix

4 eggs (never mind that the box directions say differently)

1 cup cut kernel corn (frozen, canned, or fresh)

Milk as necessary to mix (if using canned corn, use the liquid instead of milk)

Melt ¼ cup butter into a 9 x 13-inch baking dish and reserve. Mix the muffin mix, eggs, corn, and enough milk or liquid to make a thick batter, and pour over butter in baking dish. Bake at 400 degrees F. for 20 to 25 minutes. Yields 8 to 12 reasonable size portions or 4 to 6 unreasonable size portions. Serve hot for best results and rave reviews.

Here's another tip, a Word of Wisdom insight. What does it mean to eat "fruits and vegetables in their season" when you live in a large city or anywhere other than a farm? How does this apply to Latter-day Saints in this current day? If you consider that whatever is "in season" is available in abundance, then the city dweller need only look at the food ads for the local supermarket. If it's on sale, it's in season!

GREEN BEANS

BY MAUREEN URSENBACH BEECHER

It must have been the beans. I hated green beans—
cooked, frozen, but most of all, bottled. And to have to
go up and down the interminably long rows of my
mother's garden raking, hoeing, planting, weeding, and
picking the horrid things was insult beyond bearing. I
learned very early to hate gardening and everything
connected to it. Especially the beans.

We had a big backyard at our house in Calgary, but
it was all lawn. That meant that the vegetable garden
would be a vacant lot two or three blocks from home.
And big. Long rows of peas and beans to plant two
inches apart; radish and carrot and beet seeds to drib-
ble into their little ditches, then spend backbreaking
hours thinning the tiny plants—and I didn't like beet
greens, either. Lettuce to separate so it would form

heads. Spinach and Swiss chard to weed and thin. Huge Hubbard squashes to be toted home in the old red wagon and axed into wedges to be baked. No zucchini. Thank goodness, no zucchini. Had that prolific squash been around, I am certain Mother would have outdone even my Utah neighbors in dropping the unwanted extras surreptitiously on doorsteps so the recipients would have no opportunity to decline.

So when I married and we bought our own house with an equally generous backyard, I counted it a blessing that there was no garden plot. And our neighborhood was so settled that the concept of vacant lot was foreign to children and garden fanatics alike.

Neighbors, however, found spots in their yards for vegetables. Of a Saturday morning we would find on our doorstep, along with the ubiquitous zucchini, some tiny carrots from thinning, beet greens, leaf lettuce, little acorn squashes, and the crimson bliss itself: vine-ripened tomatoes.

Jaded after years of the mac 'n' cheese suppers my children preferred, my taste buds finally recovered and matured. Vegetables, steamed to a perfect crispness, bright with their own color, served in beautiful arrangement on a hot platter, have become my ambrosia. And after a Relief Society homemaking demonstration, I can bring it off myself. I offer here no recipe—the vegetables are their own best accompaniment—but a modus operandi for serving them at their peak.

The day before the big dinner, or the morning of, prepare a variety of colorful vegetables. I like broccoli, cauliflower, carrots, white turnips, and, yes, long green beans. Steam each vegetable group individually just to perfection of texture and color. Immerse immediately into a sinkful of ice water until the vegetables are cold. Strain them into their individual little bags and store them in the refrigerator. Half an hour before serving, arrange the vegetables—you get to be artsy here—on a large, heatproof platter, cover with foil, and pop it in the oven, still hot from the roast or turkey. Twenty minutes should be just right. Serve immediately. Ambrosia. Even the beans. *Especially* the beans!

RECIPES BY HEART

BY EMMA LOU THAYNE

My accordion-sided recipe holder is as tattered as memories of my mother's kitchen sixty years ago. It's what's left of my own cooking days, which have been altered in the wake of empty nesting and retirement. Not often do I bring it out these days. Even less often do I pull my mother's recipe book from the highest shelf in my study, the shelf of first editions and leather-bound rarities. This time I went for both, hunting for favorite recipes to include in this book, *Saints Well Seasoned*. Wonder. Here in my hands are not one, but two of my intimate sources of belonging. They tell me food is indeed love. In one hand I hold my mother's recipe book, with its spine gone and pages dog-eared. In the other is my 4 x 6 holder, its flap long since missing, worn thin and soggy from handling.

From the pages of the recipe book rises the succulence of Mother's plump hugs and her bread—seven loaves every other day for my father, grandmother, three brothers, and me, hot from the gas oven on bottling days in September. Standing on a flat stool to reach a steaming pot, she ladles chili sauce onto the end crust, already thick with butter. Yes. Her chili sauce comes up from the page on which she has written in pencil: *1942 nearly 2 lugs tomatoes; ¼ as many onions, made 28 quarts.*

In her artist's hand, almost like calligraphy, appear my mother's recipes for *Watermelon Pickle, Bishop's Bread, Spanish Cream, Secret Pudding, Directions for Baking and Stuffing Fish, Pop Overs, Junket.* I can taste each product and feel the process that created it. They tantalize my taste buds, activate my juices, warm my tummy (Mother never would have said anything as un-euphemistic as stomach). More, they make me smile. In them, and in all the others in those pages of hers, are family dinners, her Friday Club parties (for which we did everything but re-tar the roof), Christmas Eves and birthdays, farewells and welcomings home of my traveling father and then later my brothers.

Of course I learned to enjoy creating what could come out of a kitchen—and enjoyed, too, coming out of hers to be in my own and on my own with my 4 x 6 cards and recipes from bridal showers and neighbors, friends and Relief Societies, each labeled from where. I pull those cards out of their stuffed container, long since relegated to obscurity along with *Betty Crocker* and

Better Homes and Gardens in the cupboard over the microwave. Handling each, I spiral back through thirty years. Five daughters and I are bumping bottoms in our kitchen, following recipes, scattering spices and talk, laughing a lot, sometimes crying, being in on each other's lives, putting on a meal, making treats for picnics, creating specialities for a party or for giving away.

Some of the cards are transparent with grease, others torn with use. Some are typed, some written, the handwriting mine or the person's whose name is up in the corner: *Italian Lasagna—Kay; Fruit Siesta & Lemon Ice—Diane; Nana's Parker House Rolls; Chip Beef-Sour Cream-Artichoke Hearts—Marian; Zwieback Pie—Grandma; Dream Bars—Mrs. McLatchy,* and yep, *Bishop's Bread* (no name needed). Card after card, some sandy with remainders of crumbs and shortening, spills over in my hand with the pungence of ginger and garlic, the lick of creamed butter/eggs/sugar right off the beater, the clump of dough finding its way past fingers to a loaf tin, the soft pounding of a wooden spoon whipping white sauce, the peek at a crumb-crust topping risen in the oven to light brown and cracking out temptation.

Many of the givers of those recipes are gone, dears whose faces come up from the names in the corner to inhabit again this night of being fed from the past. I love them as I did their cooking and remember them intimately. Sunrise, sunset, one season following another, one generation bonding to another via a recipe.

My girls rush through me, all ages, all sizes, all inclinations to cook or not to cook. They have their own households now, inviting Mel and me often to them for the luxury of being cooked for. Their recipes are mostly simpler, not intended for china or silver, tasty and almost always necessarily quick. They cook well and, more often than not, without recipes. Three out of five of them live in other states and come often to visit and bring their flocks to us. Together we make meals of frozen or packaged ingredients along with pot roasts with homemade mustard and fluffy tapioca that need no reminding of how.

The 4 x 6 cards stay in their battered holder above the microwave. But I suspect that to each of those daughters, handling these cards might be what handling my mother's recipe book is to me—a gift of remembering, of savoring, of being connected, of the grace of handling the beginnings of a feast tendered into bowl and pan and oven and onto tables surrounded by the love that has made it and me and them. Out of each spills what flows in my veins and theirs. I love Emerson's, "I cannot remember the books I've read any more than the meals I have eaten; even so, they have made me." Holding these relics of meals I ate and learned to prepare, I know just how they have made us.

Take this book and fill it. Handle it and pass it along to do the same for whoever might next take it and its recipes in hand. With love, of course, with love.

ZWIEBACK PIE

Crust:

1 box unsweetened Zwieback, ground into crumbs

½ cup sugar

1 teaspoon cinnamon

Pinch salt

⅓ cup melted butter

Mix crumbs with sugar, cinnamon, and salt. Add melted butter and combine well. Use half of mixture to line a 10-inch glass pie plate; save half for topping.

Boiled custard pudding:

2 tablespoons sugar

2 tablespoons flour

2 cups milk

3 egg yolks (reserve whites for topping)

½ cup sugar (or to taste)

Vanilla and salt to taste

Mix 2 tablespoons sugar and flour in a medium bowl. Simmer milk in a small saucepan over medium heat, stirring constantly.

Remove some heated milk and add to sugar and flour mixture to moisten. Add this to remaining milk in pan and stir until thickened. Be careful not to scorch the bottom of the pan.

When milk is consistency of pudding, add egg yolks, beaten well and sweetened to taste with approximately ¼ cup sugar. Heat through (do not boil). Remove from heat and add vanilla and salt. Pour into pie plate.

Topping:

3 egg whites

⅓ cup powdered sugar

Beat egg whites until very stiff peaks form. Add powdered sugar. Pile onto custard in pie plate, covering entire top and sealing to edges. Sprinkle with reserved crumbs.

Place pie plate in a larger pan filled with water to a depth of 1 to 2 inches. Bake at 325 degrees F. for 20 minutes—or longer in slower oven—until set. The meringue will crack and probably fall after the pie is removed from the oven, but that's okay.

DREAM BARS
(Our favorite for boating trips—won't melt!)

½ cup brown sugar (packed)

½ cup melted butter

1 cup flour

Mix and press into a 13 x 9-inch pan lined with waxed paper. Bake at 325 degrees F. for 15 minutes.

1 cup chopped pecans

1 cup coconut

1 cup brown sugar

1 teaspoon baking powder

2 tablespoons flour

1 teaspoon vanilla

2 eggs, beaten

¼ teaspoon salt

Mix and spread on top of baked crust. Return to oven for about 20 minutes (until golden brown). Cut into squares.

CONTRIBUTORS

Maureen Ursenbach Beecher comes originally from Calgary, Alberta, Canada, and now lives in Salt Lake City, UT. Her literary passion is the life writings—letters, diaries, autobiographies—of ordinary women. Expressed professionally, her love led her to edit the personal writings of Eliza R. Snow, and to be general editor of the Utah State University Press series "Life Writings of Frontier Women."

Elouise Bell lives in Orem, UT. She considers herself well seasoned if not saintly. If you have bought this book, she may well have taught you or one of your children during her thirty-five years as a professor of English at BYU. She is the author of a book of light-hearted if not light-minded essays, *Only When I Laugh*.

Donna Lee Bowen of Orem, UT, is married, a step-mother of three, a grandmother of ten, a reader of murder mysteries, a weeder of gardens, and a professor of political science and Near Eastern studies at BYU.

Mary Lythgoe Bradford comes from Salt Lake City, UT, and Arlington, VA. She is the author of *Leaving Home,* a collection of personal essays (winner of AML Best Essay Award for 1987) and *Lowell L. Bennion: Teacher, Counselor, Humanitarian* (winner of the Ella Larsen Turner award for excellence in Mormon History and co-winner of the Evans Award for Best Biography of 1995).

Claudia Bushman grew up in San Francisco and has lived in seven of the thirteen original states. Currently she teaches American history at Columbia University in New York City. The author or editor of six books, including *Mormon Sisters: Women in Early Utah,* she is working on a study of a Virginia farmer.

Ann Edwards Cannon of Salt Lake City, UT, is a writer and mother of five sons. If she had hobbies, they would probably include reading, gardening, needle-pointing, and watching football. However, she has no time for hobbies right now but hopes that will change one day.

Orson Scott Card teaches the fourteen- and fifteen-year-olds in Sunday School in Greensboro, NC, where he lives with his wife, Kristine, and four children.

Delys Waite Cowles of Provo, UT, teaches English at

BYU when she is not writing books with her husband, David, sending children off to college, driving to countless music lessons and soccer games, and serving in demanding church callings. She is presently taking a nap.

Richard H. Cracroft of Provo, UT, is a professor of English at BYU and director for the study of Christian Values in Literature. He has served as bishop, stake president, and as the mission president of the Switzerland Zurich Mission.

Chris Crowe eats and writes in Provo, UT, with the help of his wife, Elizabeth, and their four children. His most recent book is *For the Strength of You: A How-To Guide for LDS Teenagers.* He keeps bread on the table by working in the English Department at BYU.

Sheryl Cragun Dame lives in Alpine, UT, with her husband and daughter.

David Dollahite of Orem, UT, is professor of family sciences at BYU and a bishop. He is co-editor (with Orson Scott Card) of *Turning Hearts: Short Stories on Family Life* (Bookcraft, 1994). He and Mary have five children.

Judy Dushku of Watertown, MA, teaches African, East European and Caribbean politics at Suffolk University in Boston. She is currently writing a book about politics in post-communist Romania. She travels with her husband, Jim, her children, and student groups to observe international political trends, and she fills her home with international students. She sometimes writes about Mormon political culture in *Exponent II.*

Mary Ellen Edmunds comes from Mapleton, UT. Besides being a "Rice Christian," she enjoys people, teaching, and writing. She is the author of *Love Is a Verb* and *Thoughts for a Bad Hair Day* as well as several talk tapes.

Eugene England lives in Provo, UT. He is married to Charlotte Hawkins England (who prefers oatmeal and makes the world's best bread). They have six children and twelve grandchildren. He teaches Mormon literature and Shakespeare at BYU and writes personal essays.

Nancy Harward moved recently from Delaware to Cincinnati, OH, where the first baptism she attended featured bagels and wildberry cream cheese. Nancy is a writer and singer, specializing in performing comic musical commentaries on LDS popular culture.

Dean Hughes is a full-time writer from Provo, UT. He has published more than seventy books for children, young adults, and adults. He is currently working on a series of historical novels about World War II called *Children of the Promise.* Deseret Book published the first two books in the series in 1997.

Kathryn H. Kidd of Sterling, VA, the author of such Mormon novels as *Paradise Vue* and *Return to Paradise,* spends as little time as possible in the kitchen. She and her husband, Clark, have probably eaten in every sit-down restaurant in Northern Virginia. Their refrigerator is full of doggie bags with contents in various stages of decomposition.

Edward L. Kimball and his wife, Bee, of Provo, UT, look to their seven children to take care of them after his retirement from teaching law at BYU, since his books on law, biography, and Church history are nearly all out of print. Happily his Sunday School president still tolerates a balding and opinionated Gospel Doctrine teacher, though the pay scale is modest.

Linda Hoffman Kimball's kitchen is in Belmont, MA. She writes many things—essays, articles, poetry, Christmas letters, and "to do" lists. Her first novel, *Home to Roost,* will not be her last. She loves dark chocolate and meals anyone else prepares.

Lael Littke comes originally from Mink Creek, ID, but Pasadena, CA, is home now. She really does like to cook when she can choose the time and menu. Three meals a day? Forget it. She'd rather be writing books for young people and children (working on number 32). As to what she'll make for dinner tonight? A reservation!

Natalie Curtis McCullough lives in Salt Lake City, UT. She is a homemaker, freelance writer, and substitute seminary teacher. Because of a rare genetic disorder, she hardly ever cooks with beans.

Louise Plummer lives in Salt Lake City, UT. She is a writer and teacher. Her most recent novel is *The Unlikely Romance of Kate Bjorkman.* She and her husband, Tom, have four sons.

Berniece Rabe calls the Denton Texas 4th Ward her home. She is the mother of four, grandmother of nine, and author of seventeen books for children. Her most recent novel, *Hiding Mr. McMulty,* is American Booksellers' Pick of the List for 1997.

Cathy Stokes grew up in Wilkinson County, MS. She now lives in Chicago, IL. She believes that our society would be improved if people sang together more. She loves to sing with groups of two or thousands. The average age of some of her very best friends is about six.

Ann Gardner Stone is an Arizona native who has been converted to the changing seasons of Evanston, IL. She still catches her breath at night at the sight of the Chicago skyline at twilight or the coral rocks of Canyon de Chelly, and will pay almost anything for a green corn tamale or Hecky's ribs. She is currently working at her third career, which causes her two sons to wonder what she's going to be when she grows up.

Emma Lou Thayne lives in Salt Lake City, UT. She is a teacher, speaker, and an author of thirteen published books, a novel, essays, stories, poems, and the words to the hymn "Where Can I Turn for Peace?" which is widely anthologized. She and her husband of forty-eight years have five daughters and nineteen grandchildren. Emma Lou was ranked number 3 nationally in Senior Women's Tennis Doubles.

Ardith W. Walker and her husband, Steve, of Provo, UT, are the parents of three children. Ardith loves teaching first grade and playing with her grandchildren.

Steve Walker of Provo, UT, is professor of English at Brigham Young University. He has published literary criticism, personal essays, and poetry, but this is his first recipe.

Bruce Young of Provo, UT, teaches English at BYU, has wide (but he hopes sane) musical tastes, and has written poetry and essays on a variety of topics. His wife, Margaret Blair Young, teaches part-time at BYU and has published novels and short stories. (Another novel, *Dear Stone,* is forthcoming.) Bruce and Margaret have four children.

INDEX